The Co-op and Basingstoke

A Story of Change

Edited by Barbara Applin

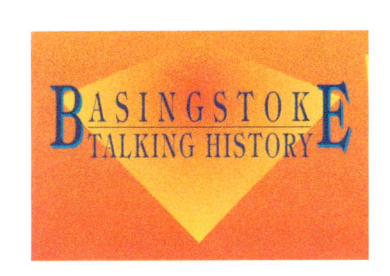

BASINGSTOKE TALKING HISTORY

© Basingstoke Talking History 2012

Published by The Basingstoke Archaeological & Historical Society

First published 2012. All rights reserved; no part of this publication may be reproduced, stored in a retrieval system, transmitted in any form or by any means, electronic, mechanical, photocopying, recording or otherwise, without the prior written permission of the Society.

A CIP data record for this title is available from the British Library.

ISBN 978-0-9508095-7-1

Line drawings by Alan Turton, Nicola Turton and Anita Leatherby

Maps by Anita Leatherby

Cover design by Sean Mullins, The Southern Co-operative

Printed by Sarsen Press, Winchester, www.sarsenpress.com

With assistance from **The Southern Co-operative**

BASINGSTOKE ARCHAEOLOGICAL & HISTORICAL SOCIETY

(Registered Charity No. 1000263)　　　　　　　　　　　　　　　　www.bahsoc.org.uk

AIMS　To investigate the history and prehistory of the Borough of Basingstoke and Deane, and to stimulate interest in archaeological and historical studies generally.

Lectures on the second Thursday of the month, from September to May, 7.30 pm at Church Cottage, Church Square, Basingstoke. Visitors welcome—£2.
Visits to places of archaeological and historical interest.
Fieldwork including fieldwalking, training excavations and finds processing.
Basingstoke Talking History—recording a wide range of memories, transcribing them and undertaking related research.

PUBLICATIONS

The Making of Basingstoke　*Eric Stokes*
Taking the Pulse of Basingstoke　*ed Barbara Applin*
Voices of Basingstoke 1400-1600　*Anne Hawker*
The Story of Basingstoke (revised)　*Anne Hawker*
Going Down Church Street to the Felgate Bookshop　*Mary Felgate and Barbara Applin*
Roundabout Basingstoke　*Barbara Applin*
Happy Christmas, Basingstoke!　*ed Barbara Applin*
The Basingstoke Riots: Massagainians v The Salvation Army 1880-1883　*Bob Clarke*

Beneath Basingstoke DVD

Quarterly *Newsletter*

FOREWORDS

Retail Co-operatives are not just about selling food and other goods to customers.

When the Basingstoke Co-operative was founded it was because a group of people existed who wanted to work with other like minded people for mutual benefit. This meant that it wasn't the actual physical setting up of that first store that was important but the philosophy behind that shop as it helped to make social changes for the better.

This interaction and support of the communities of Basingstoke and North Hampshire in which The Southern Co-operative and The Co-operative Group currently trade is a vital and integral part of their day to day business to this day.

In 1967 the Basingstoke Co-operative Society decided to merge with the larger Portsea Island Mutual Co-operative Society. With the Andover and Isle of Wight Societies also transferring in the next two years, this resulted in the creation of the first regional co-operative society in Britain.

This book is not just about shops, for in it the Basingstoke Society once more comes alive. It is about people past and present and where and how they worked and got involved with their town or village.

All too often the details of people and places are lost as a new generation replaces the previous one and this is a loss that can't be retrieved and part of our social history is gone for ever.

Thanks to this book those memories have been preserved and will be available for future generations.

Glenn Heath
Director
The Southern Co-operative

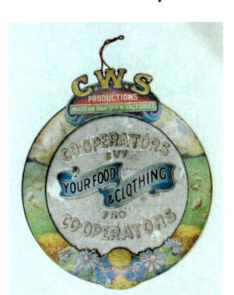

This book will enthuse local historians as the history of the Basingstoke Co-op in the 19th and 20th centuries is interspersed with many personal reminiscences of the shops, their wares and working in them.

Furthermore, the establishment of the new department store, Co-operative House, symbolised the dramatic increase of the town of Basingstoke to accommodate "London overspill" from 1961.

The text is in an appealing form with the atmosphere of the Co-op captured in a multitude of prints of contemporary sources including numerous adverts, for example from 1927 promoting soap, food, coal, overcoats and bicycles; from the 1950s marketing changed fashion for men and women, including frocks, coats and football boots; and from 1963 promoting furniture for the home and the beach. These adverts very successfully illustrate the changing patterns of commerce in the 20th century.

Women are also prominent as shop assistants and in the Co-operative Women's Guild, including the starring role of Basingstoke women in *Proof of the Pudding* entered in the Co-operative Women's Guild drama festival of 1969.

Dr Jean Morrin
History Dept
University of Winchester

ACKNOWLEDGEMENTS

We are most grateful to The Southern Co-operative for such enthusiastic support for this project. Glenn Heath and Ted Merdler allowed us to search through their archives, and Ted has given us much valuable advice. All the Co-op staff interviewed for the book have been generous with their time and keen to talk about their jobs and the co-operative ideals they follow.

On a practical level, without the help of The Southern Co-operative it would not have been possible to print this book in colour. Sean Mullins designed the striking cover, gave us initial design advice and sent us the book background for pages 28-33. We also received helpful advice on the use of the PUBLISHER software from Fred Tickle and from Maggie Donovan (DCS Computing Skills Ltd), thanks to the good offices of St Michael's Hospice, Basingstoke.

We are particularly grateful to Mark Jones, Editor of *The Basingstoke Gazette,* for allowing us to search through over a hundred years of back-numbers of *The Hants & Berks Gazette (H&BG)* and *The Basingstoke Gazette (BG)* and to reproduce so much material from them. Also to the Hampshire Record Office and the Portsmouth Record Office for allowing us similar access to their archives. Accession numbers from the appropriate archives are given throughout the book.

A huge thank you to all the people who let us use their recorded or written memories, in particular to Harold and David Griffiths for allowing us to use the extensive extract from the autobiography of Winifred Griffiths.

The Basingstoke Talking History group in the Basingstoke Archaeological & Historical Society revealed an amazing range of expertise, many members undertaking recordings and transcriptions of interviews as well as much background research to fill out the interconnected histories of the Co-op and the town. Barbara Large took photos of the records we discovered in archives and in *Gazettes* so that they could be studied at leisure; George Plummer expertly "cleaned" adverts photographed from old and sometimes tightly bound newspapers; Anita Leatherby, Alan and Nicola Turton provided the drawings which enliven these pages and Anita Leatherby drew the maps.

Thanks to the following for permission to use the photos listed below:

Bob Applin pages 29, 49, 75, 84, 113 (top), 131 (centre and bottom)
Basingstoke & Deane Borough Council pages 11, 14, 76
Basingstoke Gazette pages 77 (top), 83 (bottom), 84 (bottom), 85, 86, 110 (bottom) 112 (bottom)
Basingstoke Talking History page 3 (bottom), 4, 12, 21, 29, 42, 61, 62, 72, 78 (bottom), 79, 90, 96, 114 (left), 118, 120, 121, 123, 124 (top), 126 (bottom), 127, 128, 130, 131 (top),138
Beamish Museum pages iii, 55
A Bearne page 83 (centre)
Paul Bosley page 110 (centre)
Brookvale Community Association page 113 (3)
Robert Brown page117
Jako Carstens page 126 (left)
Harold & David Griffiths pages 28, 33
HCMS pages 10, 26, 34, 40, 74, 77 (bottom), 78 (top right), 81 (top), 82 (bottom). 87
Hampshire Record Office page 55
Joan Mussellwhite page 56
Mary Oliver page 51
Sid Penney page 5
George Plummer page 58
Debbie Reavell page 27
The Southern Co-operative Archives pages 1 (right), 54, 81 (left), 95, 109, 112 (centre), 114 (right), 119, 122, 124 (bottom)

CONTENTS

FOREWORDS	*Page iii*
ACKNOWLEDGEMENTS	*Page iv*
MAP	*Page vi*
INTRODUCTION	*Page 1*
WHY DID THE CO-OP COME TO BASINGSTOKE?	*Page 7*
THE EARLY YEARS	*Page 11*
THE FIRST WORLD WAR CHANGED PEOPLE'S LIVES	*Page 28*
BETWEEN THE WARS	*Page 39*
THE THIRTIES	*Page 53*
WARTIME AGAIN	*Page 65*
AFTER THE WAR AND THE FIFTIES	*Page 69*
THE SIXTIES	*Page 88*
THE SEVENTIES	*Page 106*
THE EIGHTIES AND NINETIES	*Page 115*
INTO THE 21ST CENTURY	*Page 120*
LOOKING BACK AND LOOKING FORWARD	*Page 130*
INDEX	*Page 136*

Basingstoke and its Co-operative Stores

Those in green no longer exist.

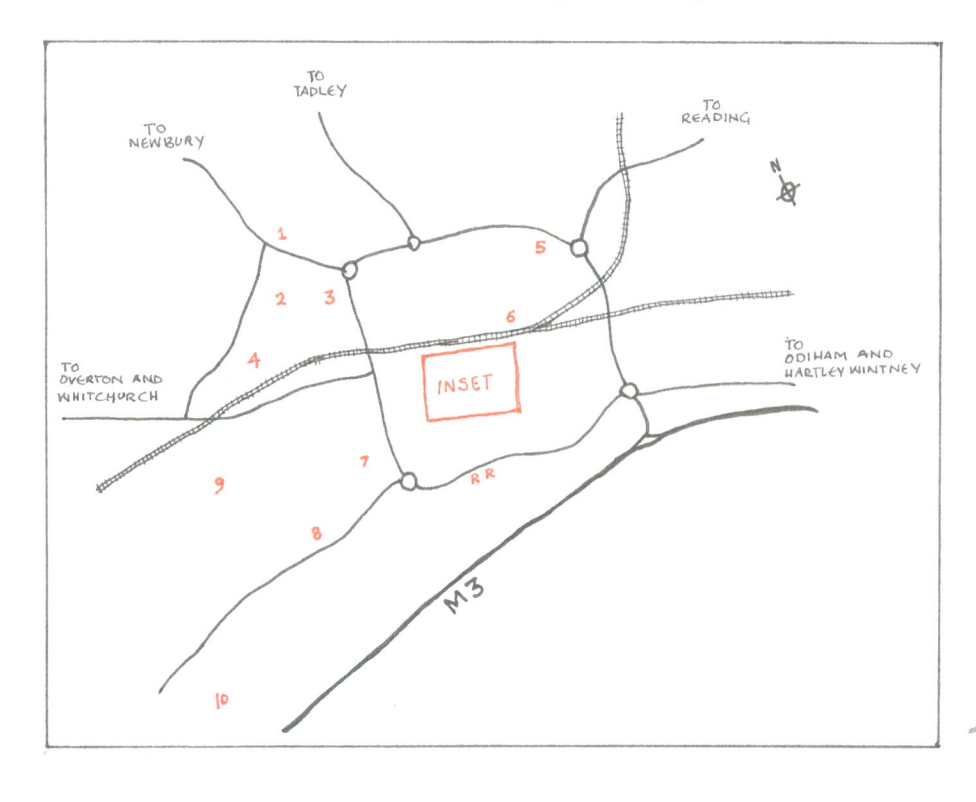

1	Rooksdown
2	Elmwood Way
3	Winklebury Way
4	Winklebury Centre
5	Oakridge Road
6	Soper Grove
7	King's Road, South Ham
8	Funeralcare
9	Buckskin
10	Beggarwood

— Railway

RR   Ring Road

Inset

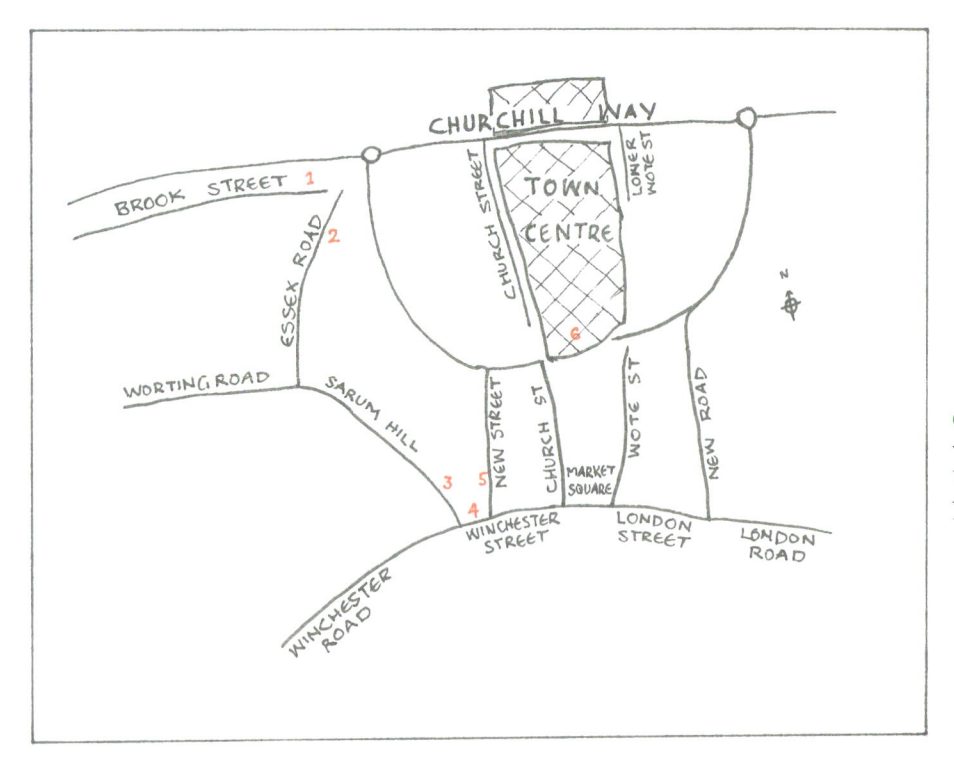

1	Brook Street (site of)
2	Essex Road
3	Sarum Hill
4	Winchester St
5	New Street
6	VISTA

Co-operative House was on the corner of Winchester Street and New Street

Sketch maps, not drawn to scale

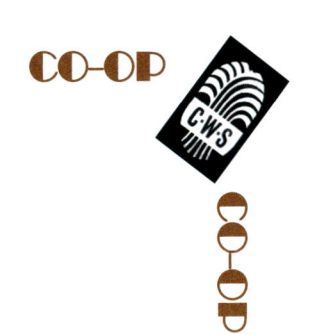

INTRODUCTION

This book began as a collection of extracts from interviews recorded for the Basingstoke Archaeological & Historical Society (BAHS) in its **Basingstoke Talking History** project. Memories of Basingstokers and incomers to the town are interesting for listeners and readers today and they will also be a valuable historical resource for the future. Many of them highlight pivotal moments in the way our town has changed over the years, as well as showing how Basingstoke took its part in national and international events.

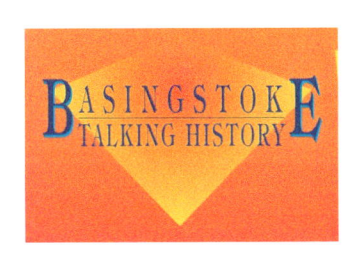

The interviews cover a wide range of topics: family stories, schools, games played, where people worked, health-matters, Christmas memories, leisure activities, wartime – and, of course, describing the old Basingstoke and its shops, the tremendous upheavals of the 1960s "redevelopment" and more recent events. Many people talk about changes in shopping habits, from small shopkeepers to supermarkets, and they often speak with affection of "The Co-op" - not just the shops where people work or buy goods, but the Co-operative Movement which set them up and its ideals of sharing and working together in a community. The Basingstoke Co-operative Society played its part in the social and economic life of the town over the years.

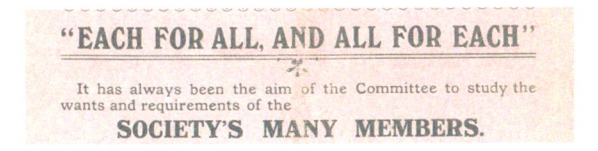

The Co-op came to Battledown Farm.
Tilly White

> The old Co-op was very good. A man would come once a week with a pony and trap and they brought the bread and flour. My sister and I used to run out and find a fancy cake as a treat. They were good. They looked after us, the old Co-op.

I was a provision hand.
Ken Toop

> There were a lot of grocers in Basingstoke, but the Co-op, I think, had the biggest organisation here. Their stuff was reasonably priced and you had the dividend, this was the thing. You felt that you were getting part of the profit back.

I was in the Furnishing Department.
Alan Andrews

> It was a great place to work. The staff were like a second family, all very good people.

As well as recording interviews, we took photographs of reports and adverts in over 100 years of back numbers of the *Hants & Berks Gazette* (*HBG*), which became *The Basingstoke Gazette* and eventually *The Gazette*. Some of the old pages are now fragile and creases could not be avoided, as happened at the top of the advert on the right. Reports of annual meetings and events give a glimpse of the early years of our Co-op but this is bound to be rather incomplete, so if anyone can add more details the BAHS will be glad to hear of them. An account in the *Hants & Berks Gazette* of the opening of the Co-op dairy in 1933 mentions the presence then of the original members number one and number two of the Society, "which was started about 40 years ago [1892], a meeting being held in a shed near the G.W.R. Yard" (in Brook Street). But was that the real beginning? See page 8.

The Basingstoke Co-operative Society soon received advice from other nearby societies and in 1899 they held an exhibition of goods made and sold by the Co–operative Wholesale Society (CWS) which had its own factories. Surprisingly, the CWS had decided not to spend money on advertising, but to use it for supplying better quality goods. Gradually adverts did begin to appear in annual reports but they didn't just show the goods for sale and the Christmas Club, as many other shops did at the time; instead they

"Membership is open to all classes" so how many MPs decided to join?

Was it a sense of civic duty that led four of the Co-op staff to become Mayors of Basingstoke?

JOIN THE CO-OPERATIVE STORES

National Co-operative Propaganda Campaign

Co-operation now has Five Million Members, representing Twenty Million people.

See its Extensive Shops and Efficient Service.

See the QUALITY, PURITY, and Neat Packing of C.W.S. Productions.

See the Dividends paid on Purchases.

See the Free Insurance based on Purchases Made—Not Premiums Paid.

Co-operative Assets: £196,350,656.
Sales: £295,828,010.
Dividends: £18,000,000.
C.W.S. Bank Turnover: £612,439,658.

All classes are joining Co-operative Societies. Manual Workers, Members of Parliament, Professional Men—and their Wives. Why not you?

JOIN NOW

— THE —
FACT OF MEMBERSHIP
IMPLIES

CONDITIONS. — Due observation of Rules. *Vide* New Special Rule VI., General Rule 107.

DUTIES . . . — Loyalty to the Trading Departments—sustained interest in our work.

PRIVILEGES. — Buying your goods Wholesale—distributing yourselves.

It was not until the late 1920s that many adverts appeared for specific products. From then on they gave plenty of information about changing tastes, needs and desires over the years.

A real gem of a discovery was the detailed description by Winifred Griffiths of her experiences working in Basingstoke's Co-operative Stores during the First World War, and her understanding of the aims of the Society. We are grateful to her son and grandson, Harold and David Griffiths, for giving us permission to reproduce her photographs and a lengthy extract from her autobiography (see pages 28-33). This shows the impact of the War on shop assistants and shoppers in our town and Winifred's awareness of the strong social and political basis of the aims of the Co-operative Movement.

MAKE SURE OF YOUR COAL DURING THE WAR

Posters and notices give a few tantalising glimpses of events at that time: there are appeals for wartime savings, mention of an allowance "in kind" to an old employee and, finally, Peace celebrations.

Newspaper reports and photographs, as well as various building plans held in the Hampshire Record Office, show how the Basingstoke Co-operative Society grew from its one shop in Brook Street into larger premises in Essex Road and then took over a succession of shop premises in New Street. Branches were also opened at Hartley Wintney, Overton and Kingsclere.

Difficulties were encountered during both World Wars and during the 1930s. In 1931 the chairman of the Society referred in particular to the economic depression and unemployment which were prevalent in the district. However, in spite of this, he said the Society's position was very sound and the returns could be looked upon as being satisfactory. He also referred to the attack made on the movement by certain sections of the press and to the agitation by private traders and others in influencing public opinion in favour of unfairly taxing Co-operative societies.

A change in policy led to a growing number of Co-op adverts in the local paper, showing a wide range of products, especially in 1938 and 1939. Then the adverts began to describe how the Co-op was helping people to prepare for difficult times. As the War progressed, Co-op adverts disappeared altogether from the local newspaper, probably because of paper shortages and maybe also as a policy decision to avoid unnecessary spending.

Searching through back-numbers and photographing adverts

After the Second World War, business grew and more premises were occupied as new departments were set up, sometimes using local architects and builders and sometimes the CWS's own architect.

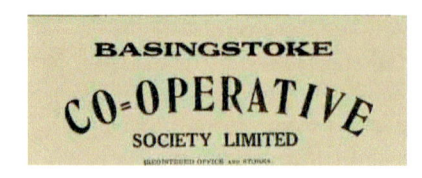

People working or shopping at the Co-op have recorded their memories, particularly of the 1950s and 1960s.

I worked on the Mutuality Club.
Joan Hobbs

> I did love that job and made lots of friends. I still talk to people in the town that I met there.

I was in the Despatch Department.
Anne Clarke

> It was all on first name terms and with none of that "I'm in charge, you will do what I say" attitude.

Many of these memories answer a range of questions about a way of life that has now disappeared.

What did a "provision hand" do?

What happened to the tokens left out for bread or milk, how was the "divi" worked out and why were Dividend Stamps introduced? How were goods delivered? Not just bread and milk but, as the Co-op's goods expanded into hardware, fashions and furniture, anything from a cushion to a three-piece suite?

Why were the "Co-op Treats" such a feature of a child's year?

How did the Co-operative Women's Guild give women a sense of fellowship and purpose? How did Basingstoke's own Guild members fare when they entered a drama competition? Minute books of the Basingstoke branch of the Co-operative Women's Guild record many varied activities over the years, sometimes instructive, sometimes entertaining.

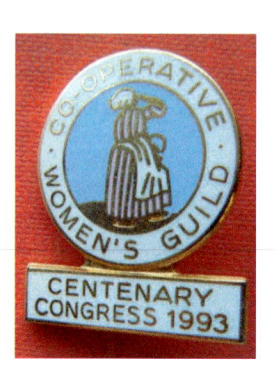

In the 1950s the town and the Co-op grew as one might expect, but in the 1960s there was suddenly a dramatic change in shopping requirements as Basingstoke experienced rapid expansion to take "London overspill". To prepare for this, in 1961 the small Co-op shops in Winchester Street and New Street and part of the stores in Essex Road were abandoned or demolished to make way for a big modern department store. This was a huge event in the town. With a growing population bringing more shoppers, the Co-op flourished and for many years Co-operative House was where customers came to buy all sorts of products, as well as to have their hair done or to stop for a cup of tea and a gossip.

Our *Wonderful*
New Promenade Store
Co-operative House

In 1967, the Basingstoke Co-operative Society became part of PIMCO (The Portsea Island Mutual Co-operative Society which had opened its first shop in Portsmouth in 1873) and so it was able to take advantage of larger resources.

PORTSEA ISLAND MUTUAL
CO-OPERATIVE SOCIETY LIMITED

Where it all started back in 1873! Our first co-op shop in Charles Street.

PIMCO itself now covered a much wider area, and became Southern Co-operatives. In 2009, more succinctly, it became

The Southern Co-operative

As Basingstoke continued to expand, and the new town centre replaced old shops, some new estates attracted Co-op shops (some of which have now disappeared). Even the grand Co-operative House closed down in 1985 and was gradually replaced by various "convenience stores", while the Co-op moved its grocery store to the town centre, naming it VISTA, but that was short-lived. And the move of the furnishing department from Sarum Hill to Winklebury was not a success.

With the growth of supermarkets the Co-op is now concentrating on improving or opening stores on the newer estates. A more recent development has been setting up Co-operative Funeralcare on the South Ham estate.

Modern methods of preparing goods, packaging and store arrangement have been introduced, with a "rebranding" to give a fresh and attractive design to shop fronts, fascias, logos, posters, leaflets, etc.

Basingstoke Talking History recordings include interviews with Co-op managers, telling of the training they received and their feelings about working for the Co-op.

Why I became Manager at Overton . . . .
    Bernard Steele

> One of the reasons that appealed to me, we're not a big, bad corporate. Our contribution to the community is really at the heart of everything we do.

Co-op staff have described their experiences of the Co-op today and their thoughts for the future, showing remarkable continuity from the original aims of the "Rochdale Pioneers" and from the early days of co-operation in Basingstoke.

For instance, in 1908 W H Brown gave a lecture *Our Native Land and the People's Share Thereof.* Today the Co-op backs Fair Trade, it encourages members to sign a petition calling for a systematic review of the impact of pesticides on honey bees and supports many "green" projects, making a point of using local suppliers where possible. In 1924 the Co-operative Women's Guild sold stamps to help miners' children and in 1929 the Basingstoke Co-operative Society donated £5 towards the cost of improvements to the X-ray equipment at the Basingstoke Hospital. Today's stores sponsor local charities, including St Michael's Hospice and RadCan and encourage their employees to do charity work in the community during their paid working hours.

The Co-operative Magazine, Summer 2010

The Southern Co-operative is an independent organisation. With its emphasis on involvement with the local community, the various stores around the town have been encouraged to develop their own individuality. Rather confusingly, the present Co-op at Winklebury is not part of The Southern Co-operative as it is one of the stores taken over recently from Somerfields by The Co-operative Group. However, the national and local societies share branding and the basic ethos and they do, as one would expect, "co-operate".

From the beginning the Co-operative societies have been "owned" by their members. Today members still have an important part to play and receive some "perks" of membership that may be little known to those who don't belong. They are invited to meetings to hear about new ventures and products, and various outings are arranged. One member has an unusual request . . .

In my Will . . .
Jo Kelly

> I've already left a little note with my Will that I want a Co-op funeral, and I do hope that somebody who's a member actually pays the bill so that they get the points on my funeral.

The Co-op has been so much a part of the social history of our town, and indeed of our country, that a display of a Co-operative Store has been set up in Hampshire's Living History museum, Milestones, and a Co-op milk delivery lorry is among the historic vehicles that have been restored.

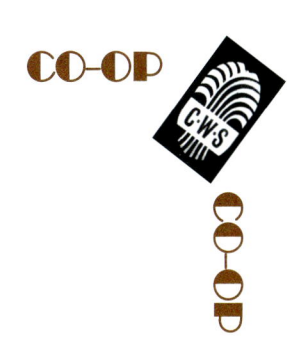

WHY DID THE CO-OP COME TO BASINGSTOKE?

> ... New Town Hall (1834) ... Corn Exchange (1865) ... Population 5574 (1871) ...

What was Basingstoke like before the Co-op came? It had been a market town since medieval times, with a good range of trades. In 1516 traders who broke the local regulations were reported to the courts and fines were imposed on bakers, butchers, fishmongers, mercers - who sold everything from threads to spices - as well as drapers, tailors, glovers, barbers, shoemakers, hosiers and cappers (who made caps). We don't know about the law-abiding tradesmen who were not recorded!

...a wide range of traders...
Joy Needham

> As a librarian, I often referred to Basingstoke's trade directories. *The Universal British Directory* for 1793 lists a wide range of traders. The Mayor then was John Ring, joiner and cabinet maker. Basingstoke had a bacon factor, bakers, butchers, a fishmonger, a fruiterer, grocers, cordwainers, drapers, a hatter, milliners, a linen-draper, breeches-makers, mantua-makers, peruke-makers and stay makers.
>
> A bacon factor was a man selling bacon, a cordwainer made shoes and boots, a mantua was a loose gown, a peruke was a wig and a stay was part of a corset.

Trading and business flourished as transport to and from the town was improved by turnpike trusts, the Basingstoke Canal and the railway (London to Basingstoke 1839, through to Southampton the following year). A new Town Hall was built in 1834 and a grand Corn Exchange in 1865.

The first Co-operative Society had been formed in Rochdale, Lancashire, in 1844. At first the Society's shops sold a limited range of basic goods to its members, They received profits, called the "dividend", in proportion to the amount of money each had spent.

The Co-operative Wholesale Society (CWS) was set up in 1863, owned and controlled by the retail societies working together. At a time when flour was often adulterated with plaster of Paris, and butter with other fats coloured yellow, the Co-op soon gained a name for the quality of the CWS brand goods sold These included items like boots and shoes, tea and chocolate, soap and furniture. Many of them were made in CWS factories. The CWS also owned and operated steam ships which imported produce from around the world, notably tea grown by co-operatives in Ceylon (now Sri Lanka).

The first Co-op shops were staffed by volunteers and only opened in the evening. When permanent staff were employed full time, their terms and conditions were better than many employees in other shops could expect. It was the Co-op who pioneered half-day closing to give shop assistants a mid-week break. As time passed, various Co-operative societies established their own butcheries, bakeries and dairies. The principles and aims of the Co-operative Movement were suggested by trade names like "Beehive" and "Wheatsheaf" to represent industry and wholesomeness.

A Co-op for Basingstoke

Although the *Hants & Berks Gazette* reported on the first meeting of the Basingstoke Co-operative Society in 1892, an attempt to set up the Co-op in Basingstoke had been made much earlier. Well before the *Gazette* itself came into existence, there was an announcement under "Basingstoke" in the *Reading Mercury*. The year was 1866.

> **CO-OPERATIVE SOCIETY** – Active measures are being adopted by the working men of this town for gaining a co-operative society for their mutual benefit, so as to procure, at the best market, groceries, bread, meat and other provisions. Whether this town is large enough to support with success such a scheme, time will show. A large number of mechanics and others have entered their names as shareholders, and it is understood the society will shortly be so far matured as to commence practical operation.

Reading Mercury 27.1.1866 HRO 98M89/Z20/13

The "mechanics" were probably employees of the metal working (mainly foundries), coach building and timber working enterprises in the town.

On 11th August the *Reading Mercury* reported that The Basingstoke Industrial Co-operative Society had held a tea and public meeting in the new Corn Exchange, when about 400 people, "members and their wives etc" sat down to tea. The chairman, Mr J Schofield (who was probably the Mineral Water Manufacturer and Coal Merchant of that name) congratulated the society upon the success they had achieved "notwithstanding considerable difficulties and opposition" and "remarks of an encouraging nature" were given by Mr A Wallis and Mr C J Steevens (later to be directors of Wallis & Steevens, the firm of agricultural engineers). Most people stayed on for the dance in the Corn Exchange "for which that building is so well adapted". It is perhaps worth noting that Mr Wallis and Mr Steevens were both Quakers.

The *Hampshire Chronicle* also reported Basingstoke news, including on 10th November that year an account of the annual meeting of the Southern Counties Adult Education Society where Mr Hobbs gave a paper on "The Co-operative Principle". He had just taken over some of the business of J B Soper, of the Basingstoke Iron Works.

The Basingstoke Co-operative Society (without the term "Industrial") was listed as an unendowed society in the Balance Sheet of Certain Societies and Charities in the Town of Basingstoke for the year 1866, edited by the Rev J B W Woollnough, curate of St Michael's : "This society has been formed in order to enable its members and others to buy food cheaply. A sum of money has been raised and a shop opened. The available balance on December 31st 1866 was £51 2s. 9d. It would appear that the moneys paid for goods during the year amounted to about £5000." It would also appear that at least one extra "0" has slipped in! *(BWM 2010.125)*

However, the next mention of The Basingstoke Co-operative Society is of its demise, with no reason given. The *Reading Mercury* of 9th July 1870 reported the proceedings of the County Court: "The Basingstoke Co-operative Society applied for leave to wind up its affairs, in accordance with the provisions of the Act, which was granted." Presumably "the Act" was the Industrial & Provident Societies Act of 1862 which had given co-operatives a corporate status for the first time and would include provisions for winding up affairs.

Many traders took up civic duties. In 1874-5 the Mayor was William Pistell, plumber; the following year it was the turn of Thomas May, brewer. Aldermen and councillors included an ironmonger, a watchmaker, a chemist, a grocer and the owner of a musical repository. The Hampshire Museums Service has a collection of Basingstoke billheads from a variety of shopkeepers throughout the 19th century, many of them offering generous credit terms. It is a pity that the lower parts of the bills showing what was bought, and for what price, were usually torn off "in the interests of confidentiality", but the headings themselves often illustrate the shops or a range of goods and are valuable examples of typography and illustrations of the time.

By the end of the 19th century there were Co-operative societies all over the country, each owned by its members. The nearest to Basingstoke was PIMCO (Portsea Island Mutual Co-operative Society) set up in 1873.

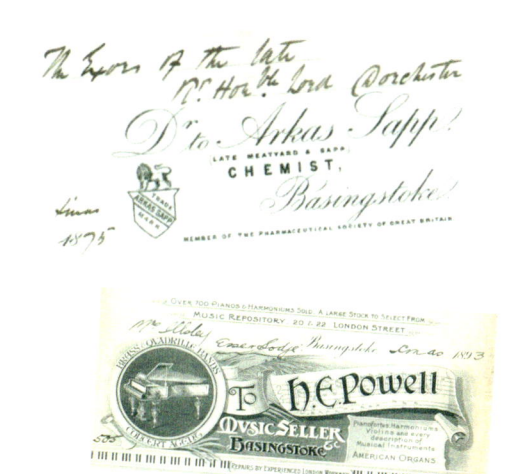

THE LADIES' CO-OPERATIVE SUPPLY ASSOCIATION (LTD)

In 1880 there were again hints that Basingstoke was interested in co-operative ideas. On February 7th, and again on 14th, the *Hants & Berks Gazette* carried an extensive Prospectus for 7 per cent preference shares of the Ladies' Co-operative Supply Association (Limited). This was apparently a national body which had a registered office in London, where they had great plans.

> The Association have in view extensive Premises situate at the West End, which are most eligible for carrying on its business. A Special Department will be set apart for the reception and Sale of Oil Paintings, Water-color Drawings, all kinds of Art, fancy and plain Needlework executed by Lady Shareholders. On all sales effected only a small commission will be charged.
>
> In connection with the Association, it is proposed to establish a School of Cookery, under the management of Miss C. H. Prichard, who holds a 1st Class Diploma, and Certificate from the South Kensington School of Cookery; also 1st Class Certificate in Cookery from the Society of Arts. Lady Shareholders would be entitled to lessons in Cookery upon specially advantageous terms.
>
> For the convenience of Shareholders, suitable Rooms for Refreshment, Reading, Writing, &c, will be provided, and a Register will be kept of the names of English and Foreign Professors, Governesses, and Tutors, Housekeepers, Lady-Helps, Domestic Servants &c, seeking engagement.

They intended to have an amazing variety of goods.

> Groceries and Provisions, Fruit, Poultry, Dairy Produce, Fancy Goods, Ormolu, Glass, China, Brushes and Combs, Baskets, Perfumery, Boots and Shoes, Furniture, Carpets, Turnery, Bedding, Sewing Machines, Leather Goods, India-rubber and Waterproof Goods, Pianos and Harmoniums, Miscellaneous Musical Instruments, Music, Electro-plate, Jewellery, Clocks, Watches, Cutlery, Drugs, Toys, Optical Instruments, Parasols, Umbrellas, Perambulators, Photography, Coloring of Photographs, Artists' Colours, Artists' Materials, Books, Stationery, Domestic Machinery, Gloves, Hosiery, General Drapery, Baby Linen, Shawls, Millinery, Ribbons, Feathers, Flowers, Furs, Lace, Moire Antique, Satins, Silks, Velvets, Fancy Dress Materials, English, Scotch and Irish Home-spuns, French and Saxon Woollen Materials, Velvet and Fancy Costumes, Bridal Dresses, Bridesmaid's Attire, Court Robes, Reception Dresses, Evening Toilettes, Dinner Dresses, Walking Dresses, Mantles, Opera Cloaks, Robes de Chambre, Carriage Dresses, Habits, Special Departments for the Handiwork of Shareholders, &c, &c, &c.

So far as practicable, Superintendents of the several Departments, and the Staff of experienced Assistants will consist of Ladies, thereby providing another opening for Female employment, a subject which has for some time past been under the consideration of a large portion of the community. A very celebrated man says, "Society is to be reconstructed on the subject of woman's toil. A vast majority of those who would have woman industrious shut her up to a few kinds of work. My judgment in this matter is, that a woman has a right to do anything she can do well. *** It is said, if woman is given such opportunities, she will occupy places that might be taken by men. I say, if she have more skill and adaptness for any position than a man has, let her have it! She has as much right to her bread, to her apparel and to her home, as men have. *** I demand that no one hedge up her pathway to a livelihood."

This was a Ladies' Association (for the well-to-do), promoting the rights of women.

Why didn't they explain it?
George Plummer

I discovered these 1880s adverts in the *Hants & Berks Gazette*. Tantalisingly, they don't explain just what was meant by "Co-operative" here.

It was another twelve years before Basingstoke again established its own Co-operative Society in 1892. Were these clothing stores another early attempt or were the advertisers simply using a term that was beginning to "catch on"?

The Basingstoke Co-operative Clothing Supply Stores open their doors on Saturday 2 October 1880, in Winchester Street.

BASINGSTOKE CO-OPERATIVE CLOTHING SUPPLY STORES
Are conducted solely upon the Cash system
And from this rule the Manager is forbidden to make Any departure

Cash versus Credit   Try the Stores for OVERCOATS
Cash versus Credit   Try the Stores for SUITS.
Cash versus Credit   Try the Stores for HATS.
Cash versus Credit   Try the Stores for GLOVES
Cash versus Credit   Try the Stores for TIES.
Cash versus Credit   Try the Stores for COLLARS.

HBG 11.12.1880

What did a Sultan boy's suit look like?

BASINGSTOKE CO-OPERATIVE CLOTHING STORES, WINCHESTER STREET, BASINGSTOKE.
ESTABLISHED FOR THE SUPPLY AT LOWEST PRICES FOR CASH ONLY, OF
BOYS', YOUTHS', & MEN'S CLOTHING, HATS, HOSIERY, &c.

THE STOCK COMPRISES
SEVERAL HUNDRED OVERCOATS,
BOYS', YOUTHS' AND MEN'S, IN
NAP, BLACK, BLUE, AND GREY DIAGONAL CLOTH, TWEED, BEAVER, PILOT, &c.
A splendid assortment of MEN'S SUITS in all the leading styles, and fashionable materials for the present season.

THE JUVENILE DEPARTMENT
Has very Special Attention.

BOYS' SUITS IN GREAT VARIETY.
In the following fashionable styles:
The CHELTENHAM, The NORFOLK, The SANDRINGHAM, The SAILOR, The CAMBRIDGE and SULTAN, &c.

AN IMMENSE
STOCK OF YOUTHS' SUITS,
The HARROW, The RUGBY, The ETON, &c., &c.

THE CHEAPEST ESTABLISHMENT IN BASINGSTOKE FOR
HATS, TIES, COLLARS, HOSIERY, & GLOVES.

Prices are not quoted, but the public are particularly requested to compare every article sold at these Stores, both for price and quality, with those purchased under the old system of business.

CASH ONLY.

NOTICE!!!
BASINGSTOKE CO-OPERATIVE
CLOTHING
SUPPLY STORES,
WINCHESTER STREET.

THE ABOVE
WILL BE OPENED
ON
SATURDAY, OCT. 2,
WITH A
LARGE AND FASHIONABLE
STOCK
OF
MEN'S AND BOYS'
CLOTHING,
HATS AND CAPS,
SCARVES & COLLARS,
HOSIERY AND GLOVES,
&c., &c.

Prices are not quoted as no correct estimate of value can be formed from them.

COME AND JUDGE FOR YOURSELVES.

CASH ONLY.

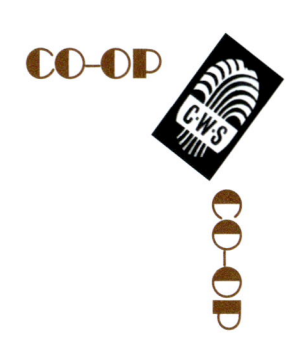

THE EARLY YEARS

1892-1914

... Population 7960 (1891) ... Typhoid epidemic 1905 ... Populaition 11540 (1911) ...

The first year

1892 is officially acknowledged as the start of the Basingstoke Co-operative Society. In March that year the *Hants & Berks Gazette* reported that Mr Frankling, of Portsmouth, visited Basingstoke to explain to interested members of the public what the Co-operative Movement was and to give advice on starting a Co-operative Store.

> A public meeting was held in the Assembly rooms, Church-lane, on Wednesday evening. The attendance was small. The chair was taken by Mr. T. Carter, secretary of the Reading Co-operative Society. Mr. Sutherland, representative of the Co-operative Wholesale Society, and Mr. A. Randle, representative of the Co-operative Society, having addressed the meeting on the advantages of co-operation among the industrial classes, Mr. Wallis asked what rate of interest was paid in the Woolwich and Portsmouth societies. The chairman said he did not know about the Woolwich society, but at Portsmouth they paid five per cent, Mr. Wallis thought that was a small amount. He said he was a strong advocate of co-operation. He asked if the society could not make arrangements with some tradesman to supply them with goods that they would not keep themselves at a reduced rate. Mr. Sutherland said it was the intention of the society to make arrangements with a baker to supply them with bread until they got a bakery of their own, and for other goods which they would not at first sell.
>
> *HBG 2.7.1892*

It is not certain where the Assembly Rooms were, possibly a building in Cross Street that had been added to the former Bluecoat School, and was accessed from Church Lane.

Unusually, the report does not give the Christian name or even the initial of Mr Wallis. This was probably the Arthur Wallis, mentioned in 1866, who founded the firm that was to become Wallis & Steevens, manufacturers of agricultural equipment. He had been Mayor four times by 1884. Or it could have been his nephew, Richard Sterry Wallis, who was to be the architect for the new stores in 1898.

Arthur Wallis

The *Hants & Berks Gazette* also reported on the first quarterly meeting on 22nd November that year, held at the British Workman in Potter's Lane. This was a public hall and temperance restaurant. About 50 members were present. It was announced that "The sales during the past quarter have amounted to £498, which, after paying all working expenses, leaves a net profit of £18, which will suffice for a dividend to members of 1s on each £1 purchases, and 6d. to non-members."

More advice

The following February, a social evening was held at the British Workman. The *Hants & Berks Gazette* of 14th February 1893 reported that between 60 and 70 members and their wives sat down to tea at seven o'clock, followed by a meeting. It was reported that the takings for this quarter came to £527 19s 11d and it was thought the dividend would be quite as high as it was before.

Mr Frankling (who had given advice on setting up the Basingstoke Store) said he was glad to see that the Society was flourishing. In what the *Hants & Berks Gazette* reporter called "a lengthy and pithy speech" he advised members, if they had any complaint, not to go talking about it to their neighbours but to go "sharply" to the Committee, and then, if they could not get an answer, to press the question at the quarterly meeting. This may suggest that there had been initial mutterings in Basingstoke or perhaps Mr Frankling was giving a warning based on experience elsewhere.

He was glad that the Basingstoke Co-operative Society had made a beginning with the bread, for while they made from 15% on their groceries and provisions, they would find that they could often make over 25% on bread and flour. He hoped that the time was not far distant when they would have an oven of their own. It seems that somebody must have asked how bread was made at the Portsmouth bakery because then he explained that the flour was mixed by the patent kneaders, and the bread was not touched by the hand till it was ready to be delivered to the customer. He added that the inside of their bakery was as clean as it was possible to be, because their fire-places were outside the bakehouses.

An aid to thrift

He reminded the members that a Penny Bank would soon be started at the stores, where they could pay in from 1d up to 5s per week, for which the Society would pay interest at the rate of 4%. He added that he hoped that parents would encourage their children in "this aid to thrift".

Meal tickets

At first the Basingstoke Co-operative Society had to make arrangements with other traders to supply items like bread and meat until they had their own bakeries and butchery departments.

> **CO-OPERATIVE SOCIETY, LIMITED.–**
>
> On and after to-day, Friday, April 21st, the following butchers, Messrs. Loveridge, and Andrews, Wote Street, the Stores, Junction Road, and the English and Colonial Meat Company, Newtown, will supply members (only) of the above society with fresh meat giving checks to the amount of their purchases, and the same rate of dividend will be paid on checks as on those received at Stores, at the end of quarter. Members are requested to call at Stores for meat tickets. Application to become a member to be made to the manager at the Stores. Sales last quarter, ending April 15th, £558.—M. BUNTING, Secretary.

HBG 22.4.1893

Junction Road had been built the previous year, leading from Station Hill to Chapel Street. Newtown was the area which had been built in the 1870s, mainly for railway employees, in Lower Brook St and May Street.

A rousing address

The quarterly meeting in September that year, again at The British Workman, was only attended by about thirty, "including half a dozen members' wives", whose presence inspired the speaker to a rousing speech and a vision of the future. The *Hants & Berks Gazette* reported that Mr Powell of Rochester, a member of the Co-operative Wholesale Central Board, "commended the Basingstoke Co-operative Society for taking the ladies into their confidence and allowing them to attend and take part in the business meeting. He thought that the more this was done the better it would be for the Co-operative Movement . . . he was inclined to think it was the Co-operative Movement that first brought the ladies into prominence, gave them some relief from the drudgery of their home life and brought them somewhat towards an equality with the men. The reason he thought the future of the Co-operative Movement rested a great deal with the women was that he knew that mothers were prepared to make sacrifices for their children; and if they in the Co-operative Movement were not prepared to sacrifice something in the present for the benefit of future generations and with the prospect of a future harvest, they would remain just where they were."

Mr Powell expanded on the benefits of belonging to the Co-operative Movement: "Their quarterly meetings brought them into association with friends, the discussion of the balance sheets added to their intelligence, the effort to grasp the figures and to thoroughly understand the question of profit and loss expanded their minds and gave them an idea of business such as was not otherwise afforded to them. The Co-operative Movement was educating the men and women of this country."

A prophecy!
Jo Kelly

> When we found this report in the *Hants & Berks Gazette* I felt I was attending that meeting myself and hearing the speaker really getting carried away with his vision of the future.

He looked forward to the time when the whole of the industries of this country would be in the hands of the workers themselves (applause); when strikes, with all their attendant wretchedness and misery, would belong to the history of the past and would be remembered only to be regretted; when profits would belong to those who made them; when the workman would receive the just reward of his toil, not as a pittance but as a right; when their children would occupy a better position than they enjoyed today; and when every family would live under their own vine and fig tree none daring to make them afraid; when there would be no spoliation, no robbery; when drones should no longer extract from the hive the honey that had been gathered by the bees; when they who did not work should not eat; when each would work for all and all for each. This grand and glorious time was coming. It might not come quick enough for their socialist friends, but they would gradually take hold of the railways, the mines, and the other great industries of the country.

HBG 9.9.1893

The report for the quarter ending July 15th last shows that the sales amounted to £582 13s. 9¼d, the profit on which was £27 13s.10d., which was appropriated as follows: 9d. Dividend on members' cheques of £1, and 4½d. Dividend on non-members' cheques of £1; the balance towards preliminary expenses.

New premises

At first the Basingstoke Co-operative Society's headquarters were in Brook Street but they had difficulty in finding a piece of land on which to build a shop until Mr Saunders of Rochford Road made available some land in nearby Essex Road.

Plans for the new Store Premises were passed on April 14th 1898. The shop was to have a boot department on the left and a trying on room, with a store behind. In the yard were a bake house and coal store. The width of the frontage abutting onto the street was to be 40 feet, the height of the building to the eaves 22 feet, the external walls of 9", 11" and 14" brick and the roof to be of slate.

HRO 58M74/BP42

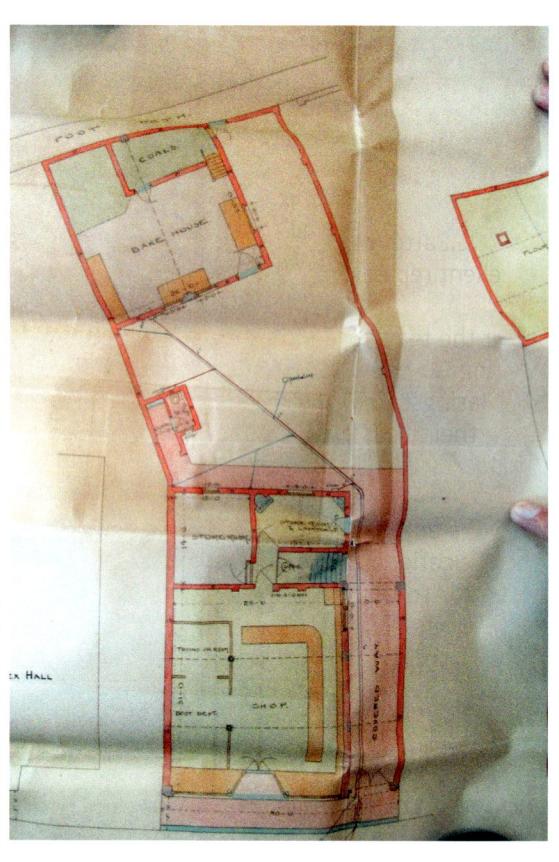

One of the two architects was Richard Sterry Wallis, who was a Borough Magistrate in 1895 and was to become Mayor in 1903.

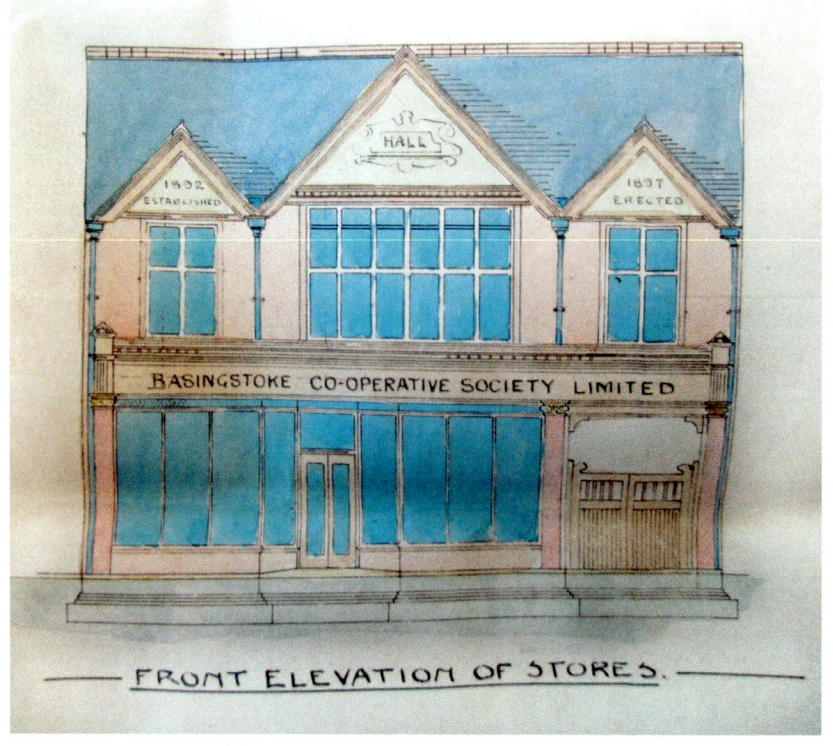

A very flourishing condition

On January 7th 1899 the *Hants & Berks Gazette* reported that the Basingstoke Co-operative Society had been forced to get out of their old stores in Brook Street at very short notice but new stores had been erected in Essex Road and "a bright, cheerful and spacious assembly hall built for the meetings of the Society." A members' tea was given in the Hall, and was well attended, "about 100 partaking of the very excellent repast provided by the Committee."

After the tea there were speeches by the chairman and visiting Co-operative Society notables. They advised the Basingstoke Society to think of getting money from their Union for building cottages for workmen "because Basingstoke was increasing in population and working men were coming into the town and would do so more and more." They were advised to make use of the educational fund to educate and train their children "so that they could take the part they ought to take when they became men in the government of their country". And members were advised to make all their purchases at their own stores.

Mrs Holmes, the Secretary of the Portsea Island Women's Guild, naturally suggested Basingstoke should form a Women's Guild. This could organise sick-nursing classes, first aid to the wounded, and so on. The reference to "the wounded" reflects the likelihood of war. The Battle of Omdurman had taken place in the Sudan the previous year, and at this time there was unease leading to the second Boer War. It is interesting to see that women were beginning to make themselves felt: the International Women's Congress was to take place in London in June that year.

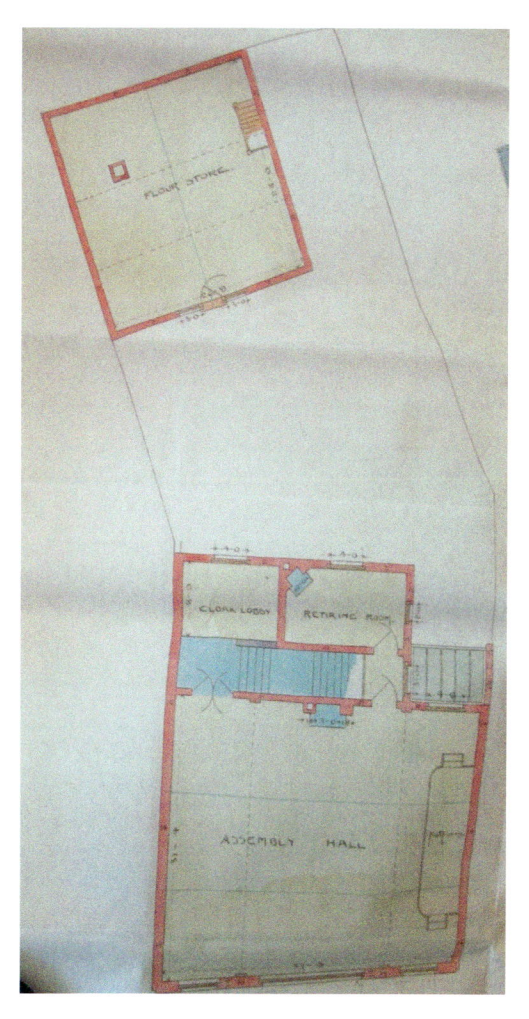

HRO 58M74/BP42

Mr Adam Dean, of the Co-operative Union, Manchester, giving "a capital speech", referred to the evils of the sweating system and the leasehold system, and the part played by trade unionism in improving the condition of the working classes. He said, "If they as co-operators were ever going to take the position they ought in the legislation of their country they could only do it by training themselves. And this was being done slowly, gradually and surely, and they were raising up men from the ranks capable of taking positions of responsibility in the government of their land . . . The great aim of each one of them should be to leave the world a little better than they found it, and to help share the burdens of their fellows."

It wasn't all pontificating, however. Between the speeches Miss Richards played a pianoforte solo, Mr Farmer sang *Good-bye, Sweetheart*, Mr Squires sang *Old folks at Home* and Miss Richards played another pianoforte solo, the waltz *Dewdrops*.

There was something for the children too.

> On Tuesday evening, about 190 children of the members were treated to a free tea, to which it is needless to say they did ample justice. After tea a very interesting lantern entertainment was given, the subject being 'The orphan children'. The lantern was manipulated by Master Edgar Wagstaff, and Mr. John White gave the connective readings. Miss S. White rendered several pieces on the piano at intervals. At the close the children gave some hearty cheers for all who had contributed to their amusement. They dispersed about 8.45.

HBG 7.1.1899

An exhibition and a conference

On 10th June that year the *Hants & Berks Gazette* reported, "With a view to the extension of the Co-operative Movement and spreading knowledge of it in this district, the Co-operative Wholesale Society gave an exhibition of goods manufactured and sold by them in the Drill Hall, on Thursday. Before the opening of the Exhibition a luncheon took place in the Masonic Hall, of which about sixty delegates from various Societies and others partook." A vote of thanks to the CWS was proposed by Mr J Redes, the chairman of the Basingstoke Society.

> After enjoying some fragrant cigars that Mr. Swain had handed round, the company adjourned to the Drill Hall, where the ceremony of opening the Exhibition took place. Around the sides of the Hall, and in glass-covered stands in the centre, were arranged articles of all descriptions, from boots and brushes to bacon and cheese, manufactured or sold by the Co-operative Wholesale Society. The string band played an opening selection, and then Mr. Russ, who acted as Chairman, rose and expressed his pleasure at seeing such a good muster, and said he hoped they would all inspect the productions of the Society. He then called upon Mr. Pumfrey to open the sale.
>
> The delegates then adjourned to the Co-operative Assembly Hall in Essex Road, where a conference took place arising out of a paper read by Mr William Openshaw of London on "Store Management".
>
> *HBG 10.6.1899*

There was a constant stream of visitors to the Exhibition in the afternoon and evening. Other speakers included Mr Carter, the Secretary of the Reading Society, who complimented the Basingstoke Society on having built such a nice store. It was quite a credit to the town. He hoped that in the course of years the Basingstoke Society would figure as one of the leading, most progressive and thorough-going societies known in the Co-operative Movement. This aspiration was met by applause from the audience. Mr R W Tutt, one of the directors of the CWS, said the Basingstoke Society of 185 members had a share capital of about £800.

Mr Tutt went on to tell members that when the Portsea Island Society was set up in 1873 they had been boycotted by other traders and suppliers who feared competition. He explained, "The Wholesale Society was formed by Co-operative societies themselves at a time when merchants refused to supply Co-operative societies for fear of offending other customers. Co-operators found they were getting into second rate markets, and in order to get out of the difficulty they made themselves entirely independent of the merchants and manufacturers by the formation of the Wholesale Society as a centre from which they could draw supplies. As the Co-operative societies found the capital for and formed this Wholesale Society it was their duty to take from it the goods which it had been formed to supply and not to get their goods from any other market. In the same way individual Co-operators should buy their goods from their own stores."

Surprises?
Ian Williams

> Reading this report, I was not surprised at the reactions of other traders but I was surprised to discover that in their early years the CWS ignored the power of advertising.

Mr Pumfrey, another director of the CWS, proudly said, "The CWS spent nothing on advertisements. The Society employed a great many hands at its soap works. One firm of soap manufacturers spent £100,000 a year in advertising. The Society saved all that, and the buyers got the benefit in the soap." He then repeated Mr Tutt's explanation of the origins of the CWS, almost word for word, adding that "It was a Society of Societies (about eleven or twelve hundred societies) which could then supply themselves with food and clothing at first hand very much better than they could in their individual capacity. The CWS employed some 1200 hands in making boots for members of their societies, and these boots could be bought nowhere but at the Co-operative Society's Stores."

At the Basingstoke Branch's AGM in 1900 Mr J E Johns, President of the Reading Co-operative Society, was the first speaker and said that there was no need to fear competition. He asked what difference it made whatever Jones sold his goods at so long at they knew they were paying a fair price at the Stores and were pocketing the dividends and profits themselves. What upset him was to see people who belonged to the Society patronising "cutting" shops and hunting for bargains in the market late at night, trying to take advantage of a man who had not had the luck to sell out before nine o'clock. He said that most of these cutting shops were worked by joint stock companies, and the profit made did not stop in their own town; "therefore they were on a very different footing to the private tradesman who lived in the town, spent his money here, subscribed to the local charities and acted as a good citizen." He went on to point out, however, that where the dividend was 2s in the £, as it was here, a man who spent 10s a week at the Stores practically increased his wages by 1s a week, "and the ladies in particular knew how far a shilling went".

Women's Co-operative Guild, Basingstoke Branch

The Women's Co-operative Guild (later called the Co-operative Women's Guild) was founded in 1883 as the women's section of the Co-operative Movement. Meetings at first covered subjects that were said to be traditionally of interest to women, such as childcare, housekeeping and needlework.

In January 1899 Mrs Holmes, Secretary of the Portsea Island Mututal Co-operative Society, suggested that the Basingstoke Society should form a branch of the Women's Co-operative Guild and by the end of September the Branch held fortnightly meetings. Mrs Adam Deans of Woolwich addressed one "well-attended meeting" in the Co-operative Society's Hall, when she was described as "an excellent speaker, clear, pointed, and bright, well qualified to take part in that educational work in the Co-operative Movement which she so earnestly advocates." She enlarged on the potential role of women in the Co-operative Movement.

> Mrs. Deans then spoke of the objects of the Women's Guild, pointing out that co-operation was a most interesting study for women. She felt that many of the evils which existed to-day in connection with production would never have existed had women had more voice in the management of affairs. No co-operative society was worth the name that did not welcome women with open arms and give them every privilege that men had got. She did not mean that they should put a woman on the Committee of Management or on the Educational committee because she was a woman. Let them nominate fit and proper persons for the post, but not put on an incapable woman before a good man, nor an incapable man before a good woman.

HBG 30.9.1899

Improvements to Essex Road

Although Essex Road was not one of the major streets of the town when the Co-op first set up premises there, by 1895 the Kelly's Directory listed 35 occupants there, including three clergymen and a builder,

The Co-op submitted a planning application, approved on 19th June 1905, for additions to their premises. On the right of the old covered way were a new shop, offices and strong room with a show room and store on the first floor. The yard now had a cart shed and a stable with a manure pit outside. The architects were Wallis (again) & Smith.

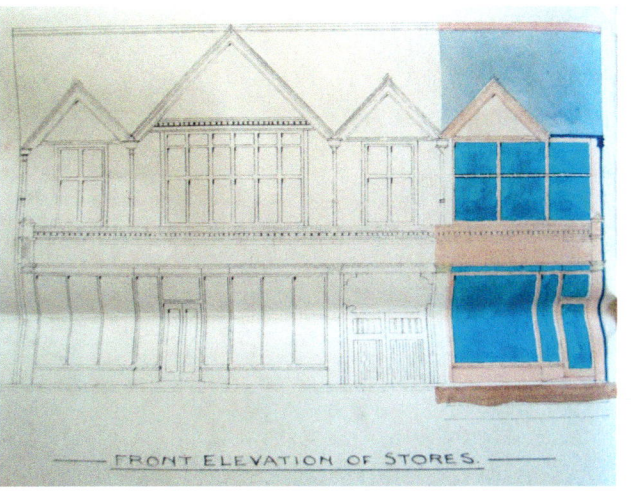

FRONT ELEVATION OF STORES.

HRO 58M74/BP360

A growing business

A stern announcement

C·W·S "WHEATSHEAF" BOOTS
BOOTS AND SHOES — 21/- — in Box Calf, Glacé Kid & Willow
ALL STYLES
Sold at Co-operative Stores Only.

The Co-op adopted the wheatsheaf as an emblem of good husbandry and prosperity.

THE FACT OF MEMBERSHIP IMPLIES

CONDITIONS. Due observation of Rules. *Vide* New Special Rule VI., General Rule 107.

DUTIES . . . Loyalty to the Trading Departments—sustained interest in our work.

PRIVILEGES. Buying your goods Wholesale—distributing yourselves.

We believe that reflection will find these features to be advantageous, rather than on the contrary.

Member's No. 3 Capital at Quarter End, £19 6 11
Store Purchases, £24 6 9 Trade Purchases, £3 14 11
Including Balance from last Quarter.

EDUCATIONAL COMMITTEE.

A MAGIC LANTERN ENTERTAINMENT,
consisting of Interesting Views, Humorous, Comic, and Moving Figures, will be given in the
Society's Hall, on Thursday, February 15th, 1906, at 7 o'clock,
By Mr. T. J. ELLINGHAM.

For young Co-operators only, from 5 to 15 years of age. Admission only by Ticket—FREE—to be obtained at the Stores, on and after Monday, February 12th. Fathers and Mothers NOT invited. The doors will be opened at a Quarter to Seven o'clock.

No parents invited!

They wanted to attract "a man with critical taste" who would look for style and quality".

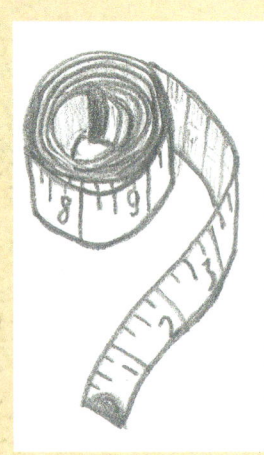

WHEATSHEAF BOOTS & SHOES.

When a Man with critical taste, looking for quality footwear, decides upon a specific brand of goods, : : : : : : :

THE REASON is because of their superiority over all others. Did you ever know a man to put his foot into a pair of WHEATSHEAF BOOTS without liking them?

SELLING GOODS that bring business is our object. A trial order means a satisfied customer.

Boot Department, ESSEX ROAD.

WHO'S YOUR TAILOR?

Wear Your Own Clothes. Not necessarily because you bought and paid for them, but more especially from the fact that they were : : : : : : : : : : : : : : :

MADE TO FIT you, embodying the many little individualisms which denote the really high class "made-to-measure" suit. Our patrons have the advantage of choice from a wide range of patterns, in which Economy, Style, and Quality have met together.

WE SHALL BE PLEASED to show you samples of materials and take your measure.

Bespoke Dept., ESSEX ROAD.

In 1907 the Co-op began selling medicines.

THE BASINGSTOKE CO-OPERATIVE STORES

In addition to their largely increasing Clothing Trade, have commenced the sale of

PATENT MEDICINES & PROPRIETARY ARTICLES

and respectfully invite attention to the subjoined list.

Item	Size	Price	Item	Size	Price
Allcock's Porous Plasters	1/1½ size for	7d	Judson's Dyes	6d size for	4d
Allcock's Corn Plasters	1/1½ ,,	9½d	Hop Bitters	4/6 ,,	2/10½
Brown's Bronchial Troches	1/1½ ,,	10d	Keating's Worm Tablets	1/1½ ,,	10½d
Bunter's Nervine	1/1½ ,,	10d	do. Insect Powder	6d ,,	4½d
Brandreth's Pills	1/1½ ,,	7½d	do. Cough Lozenges	1/1½ ,,	10½d
Beecham's Patent Pills	1/1½ ,,	9d	King's Dandelion & Quinine Pills	1/1½ ,,	9d
Braggs' Vegetable Charcoal Biscuits	1/- ,,	9d	Kay's Worsdell's Pills	1/1½ ,,	9d
do. do. do.	2/- ,,	1/6	Kay's Essence of Linseed	1/1½ ,,	10d
Blair's Gout Pills	1/1½ ,,	9d	Knight's (Squire) Eye Ointment	1/1½ ,,	10½d
Clarke's Blood Mixture	2/6 ,,	1/10½	Locock's Wafers	1/1½ ,,	10d
Cockle's Pills	1/1½ ,,	9d	Lamplough's Pyretic Saline	2/6 ,,	1/9
Cigarettes (Joy's) for Asthma	2/6 ,,	1/10	Mother Seigel's Syrup	2/6 ,,	1/10
Chlorodyne (J. Collis Brown's)	1/1½ ,,	10d	Mother Seigel's Pills	1/1½ ,,	9d
Clarkson's Embrocation	1/1½ ,,	9d	Magnesia (Dinneford's)	1/- ,,	8½d
Condy's Fluid (Crimson)	1/- ,,	8d	Magnesia (Bishops Granular)	1/- ,,	8½d
Davis's Pain Killer	1/1½ ,,	10d	Mustard Leaves (Rigollot)	1/- ,,	9d
Dredge's Heal-All	1/1½ ,,	10½d	do. do.	6d ,,	4½d
De Jongh's Cod Liver Oil	2/6 ,,	1/9	Norton's Camomile Pills	1/1½ ,,	9d
Dinneford's Fluid Magnesia	1/- ,,	8½d	Neaves' Infant's Food	1/1½ ,,	8½d
Eno's Fruit Salt	2/9 ,,	1/10	Powell's Balsam of Aniseed	1/1½ ,,	10d
Elliman's Embrocation	1/1½ ,,	10½d	Parr's Life Pills	1/1½ ,,	9d
Elliman's Embrocation for Horses	2/- ,,	1/6	Pepper's Quinine and Iron Tonic	4/6 ,,	3/9
Epps' Glycerine Jujubes	7½d ,,	5½d	Page Woodcock's Wind Pills	1/1½ ,,	9d
Fennings's Hooping Cough Powders	1/1½ ,,	10½d	Parrish's Chemical Food	2/3 ,,	1/6
do. Children's Powders	1/1½ ,,	10½d	Pond's Extract	1/1½ ,,	10½d
do. Lung Healers	1/1½ ,,	9d	Rooke's Solar Elixir	4/6 ,,	3/-
do. Stomach Strengtheners	1/1½ ,,	9d	Rooke's Oriental Pills	1/1½ ,,	9d
do. Fever Curer	1/1½ ,,	10½d	Rooke's Golden Ointment	1/1½ ,,	10½d
do. Worm Powders	1/1½ ,,	10d	Ridge's Food	1/- ,,	9d
Floriline (Gallups)	2/6 ,,	1/10	Steedman's Soothing Powder	1/1½ ,,	9½d
Frampton's Pill of Health	1/1½ ,,	9d	Scott's Liver Pills	1/1½ ,,	9d
Friar's Balsam	6d ,,	4d	Sedlitz Powders	1/- ,,	8½d
Glycerine (Perfumed)	6d ,,	4d	Savory and Moore's Food	1/- ,,	9d
Gelatine (Nelson's)	6d ,,	4d	Winslow's Soothing Syrup	1/1½ ,,	8½d
Holloway's Pills	1/1½ ,,	9d	Whelpton's Pills	1/1½ ,,	9d
Holloway's Ointment	1/1½ ,,	9½d	Welch's Pills (Kearsley's)	2/9 ,,	2/-

The range of goods increased dramatically . . .

NOTICES.

This Society supplies Boots and Shoes, Drapery, Men's and Boys' Clothing, Umbrellas; Bedsteads, Bedding, Carpets, and other Furniture; Sewing, Washing, Wringing, and Mangling Machines; Clocks, Watches, Perambulators, Bicycles, Tricycles, Harmoniums, Pianos, Books, &c., from the Co-operative Wholesale Society.

Any article required and not kept in stock can be obtained on very short notice through the Co-operative Wholesale Society, of which our Society is a member.

Even so, good relations with other traders were still necessary, as another notice makes clear.

> The following tradesmen allow discount to the Society and give checks to Members for all goods purchased for themselves or family at their respective establishments—Drapers and Clothiers: Mr. H. Jackson, Church Street; Mrs. Coleman, Wote Street; Mr. F. Boyer, London Street; Mr. J. G. Knowles, Winchester Street; Longley Bros., Church Street; Mr. J. Gammon, Winchester Street. Ironmongery (except Tools): Mr. Punter, Wote Street. Butchers: Mr. Stratford, Church Street; Messrs. W. and R. Fletcher, Winchester Street; Southern Counties Meat Co., Wote Street; Mr. Barlow, Wote Street. Member's number must be given in all cases in order to receive a check.

This notice is repeated, with minor changes, up to 1915. Did these other traders in the town regard the Co-op as a threat to their businesses and try to keep their customers by this means? From the Society's point of view it was part of the Co-operative ideal that they should co-operate not just with its members but with the whole community, including rival traders.

There were other initiatives too.

> COALS supplied in 1 cwt. and upwards. Prices on application.
>
> CO-OPERATIVE PENNY BANK AND PROVIDENT CLUB.—Payments are taken, and withdrawals from Penny Bank paid out on Saturdays, from 3 to 4 and 6 to 8-30 p.m. in Secretary's Old Office, upstairs.

> WE HAVE A VARIED STOCK OF
> **Hardware, Enamel-Ware, Brushes, Mats, and Rugs.**
>
> NOW or NEVER is the time to make your purchases.

Entertainment always had to be followed by instruction. The *Hants & Berks Gazette* for 15th January 1907 reported on "a most successful annual meeting and concert" held at the Drill Hall. "The meeting was preceded by a tea. The gathering was largely attended by working men and their wives and daughters [no sons?], the large Hall being packed." An excellent musical programme had been arranged, one singer having to compete unfortunately with "the accompaniment of a crying infant".

Some Basingstoke names will be familiar: Miss Amy Aylward (Mrs Baker) playing a pianoforte solo and Mr Wilfrid Edney providing accompaniment for one song. Miss Aylward was a piano teacher, living in Sarum Hill and Mr Edney was a furnisher (in 1915 he was in Winton Square).

> Some striking figures showing the progress of the Society's business since the original store was opened in Brook Street in 1892 were given by the Chairman. The sales the first year amounted to £498, the share capital was £146 and the profits £18. Fourteen years afterward the balance sheet showed sales amounting to £4027, profits £390 and share capital £4384. During the fourteen years of the society's existence they had paid for goods £105,581; they had paid away in wages £7,364, and in dividends £8,187. Where had these dividends gone? In some cases the money had gone to make the homes of the members more attractive and comfortable. In other cases it had helped the bread winner, when thrown out of employment, to keep the wolf from the door, and it had afforded assistance in sickness. In other cases, where the members were more fortunate, the dividends had been left in the Society and the members now had a good round sum, standing to their credit. This was one of the easiest and best methods within the reach of working men of putting by a trifle for a rainy day. (applause)

The principal address was given by Mr R Bell, MP, comparing the Co-operative Movement and Trades Unionism, and emphasising their close links. "I can venture to assure you of this, that wherever you find working men have embraced trades unionism and co-operation, there you will find in the houses of those men brightness, cheerfulness and happiness, and there you find sobriety, if not absolute teetotalism." The reporter noted "applause" at this.

From 1908 to 1910 reports and balance sheets also gave instructive information about resources and sales. The following information from the Bakery Department was followed by the rather hectoring question:

Do you support your own Bakery? IF NOT, WHY NOT?

Advertisements gave advice on **THE RIGHT WAY** and **THE WRONG WAY** to buy basic goods. Even the notice of the lecture to be illustrated by Limelight Lantern Views was followed by a discreet "hope". It would be interesting to know how many the hall held and if the lecture was interesting and well attended.

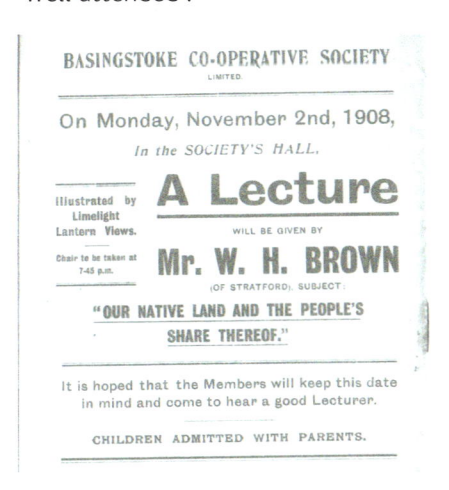

In 1910 the average weekly wage of male employees in the Co-op shops was £1 10s (£1.50) per week, while the average for females was £1.

A boy taken on as an apprentice bootmaker was paid one shilling (1s or 5p) a week. Dressmaking apprentices (always girls) started at two shillings a week.

We found boots and shoes.
Anita Leatherby

Searching through the Co-op archives, we were delighted to find boots and shoes, so out came the camera.

HBG 27.7.1907

21

THE ANNUAL TEA AND ENTERTAINMENT

WILL BE HELD IN THE

DRILL HALL, MONDAY, JANUARY 30th, 1911.

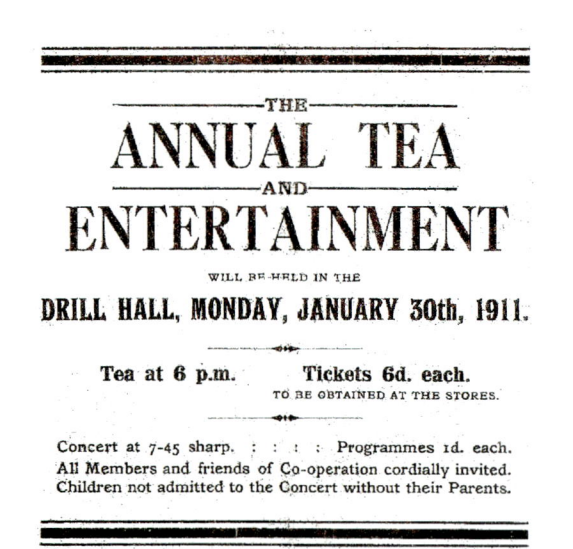

Tea at 6 p.m.   Tickets 6d. each.
TO BE OBTAINED AT THE STORES.

Concert at 7-45 sharp. : : : : Programmes 1d. each.
All Members and friends of Co-operation cordially invited.
Children not admitted to the Concert without their Parents.

As usual, this event was reported in the *Hants & Berks Gazette:* "The success of the gathering was quite unprecedented, something like five hundred being present at the tea, while for the concert which followed the Drill Hall was completely packed. The chairman contrasted this with the first gathering when about 30 members sat down to tea, and about 50 attended the meeting afterwards.

The concert included such well-known songs as Sullivan's "A Regular Royal Queen" and Cay's "I'll Sing Thee Songs of Araby" as well as "Toothache" and "Little Tommy went a-fishing". There were violin solos, a pianoforte duet and humorous sketches.

At the annual meeting the chairman reported that the Society had 30 members in Oakley, 30 at Basing and several at Herriard, Hook and elsewhere. He said that co-operation was extending in various forms: "many masters were dividing a certain percentage of their profits among the workers, which was one form of co-operation, and a most commendable one. It helped the men, and it helped the masters, as it got the best out of their men, and it encouraged the men to put all their interest into their work, and this in turn increased the profits." Farmers were also co-operating by banding together in order to sell their produce in the best market. The report concluded with a plea for members "to put their shoulders to the wheel and do all they could in the cause of co-operation, so that the year 1911 might be even better than 1910".

The following table shows comparative usage of flour and sales of flour and bread 1910-1911. The receipts from sales of cakes rose steadily from £130 19s 0d to £155 6s 8d.

Quarter ended	Flour used (sacks)	Bread sold (loaves)	Flour sold (bags)
March 1910	436	68,458	8,956
June 1910	441	71,471	8,625
September 1910	467	74,081	7,742
December 1910	499	79,301	9,177
March 1911	437½	69,503	8,172
June 1911	460½	74,441	8,238

There were several notices for the quarter ending March 27th 1911.

DID YOU KNOW?

THAT YOU COULD GET YOUR

BOYS' READY-MADE SUITS

AT THE STORES?

WE HAVE ALL SIZES IN STOCK IN GOOD, HARD WEARING TWEEDS. EXCELLENT FOR SCHOOL WEAR.

Quality Right.   Style Right.   Prices Right.

WE STRONGLY RECOMMEND

FOR THE SUMMER TRADE OUR NEW

Citrate of Magnesia, 6½d. per bottle, Sherbet, Lemon Squash, Lime Juice Cordial, Tinned Pears, Peaches, Pineapples, and Apricots.

Two years ago, we used to boast of making 1,700 loaves for Easter Saturday; this year we have made 2,123 loaves of Bread for one day only—

THANKS TO YOU.

The *Co-operative News.*—This is a penny weekly paper, the only organ of the Co-operative movement. All Members who wish to thoroughly understand and appreciate the importance and magnitude of the movement should purchase a copy weekly, which is sold at the Stores at half-price. It contains reports of meetings, chronicles the progress, expounds the principles, and illustrates the practice of Co-operation throughout the United Kingdom. It caters specially for the children, the women, and the employees, as well as for the ordinary Members. Can be obtained on and after Friday afternoons.

The Women's Co-operative Guild was now well established and advertised its conference in the Society's Annual Report.

Later the Guild changed its name to the Co-operative Women's Guild.

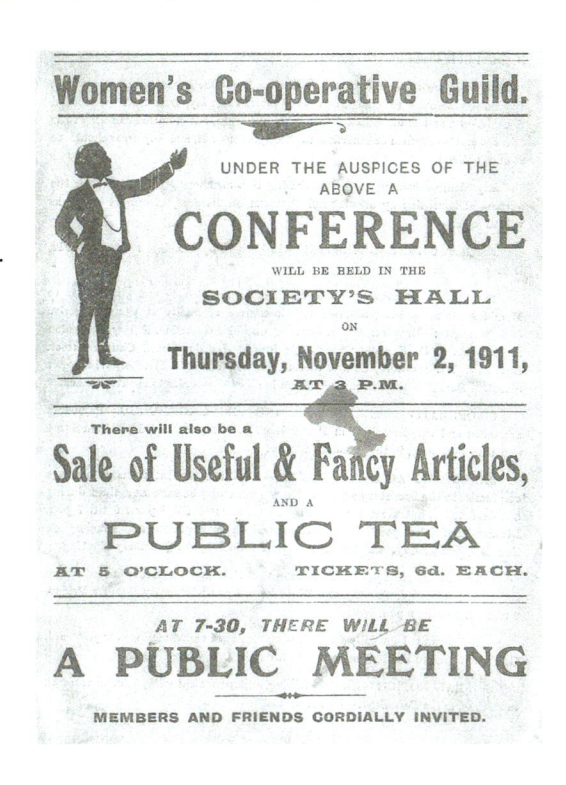

Women's Co-operative Guild.

UNDER THE AUSPICES OF THE ABOVE A

CONFERENCE

WILL BE HELD IN THE

SOCIETY'S HALL

ON

Thursday, November 2, 1911,

AT 3 P.M.

There will also be a

Sale of Useful & Fancy Articles,

AND A

PUBLIC TEA

AT 5 O'CLOCK.   TICKETS, 6d. EACH.

AT 7-30, THERE WILL BE

A PUBLIC MEETING

MEMBERS AND FRIENDS CORDIALLY INVITED.

A new building

The growing range of goods called for larger premises. At the quarterly meeting on 6th November 1911, once the normal business had been disposed of, the following motions were discussed:

> 1. That the hall be made suitable and used for business purposes.
>
> 2. That the Committee be authorised to proceed with the erection of a new building at the rear of the Grocery Department, consisting of a basement 5ft. 3in. under ground; over that a Store which it is proposed to use as an Order Department, thus relieving the congestion of the Front Shop; and above that a Store for sugar and other goods. Rough plans will be shown and further details given at the meeting.

A planning application for new stores, sanitary block and alterations at Essex Road was passed on 9th May, 1912. The architects were again Wallis & Smith. The cellar walls were to be built with a ½" cavity filled with White's Hygean Rock. By now the bake-house was shown with ovens, stoke hole and cooling room. The shop on the left of the front door was for groceries and that on the right the boot department. There were also a despatch/order room, the Manager's office and the Secretary's office. The new sanitary block was behind the stable and fodder store. On the first floor the hardware and dry store were on the left with the board room on the right and stores behind, one specifically for flour.

The Committee's reports to quarterly meetings in 1912 described this progress.

> You will observe by the Agenda of Business on another page that the Committee are desirous of increasing the sum proposed to be spent on the New Building from £1,100 to £1,200. The purpose for the additional money is that your committee, after due consideration, have decided it will be in the interest of true economy and up-to-date efficiency to install a modern Heating Apparatus for the two Stores, the Despatch and Hardware Departments, the Offices and the Board room. You can rely on your Committee seeing that no money is spent in waste, and that value is received for what is expended.

THE NEW BUILDINGS

> An extension of the society's premises are being carried out, the Grocery Department has been enlarged by the addition of a cellar, despatch room, and store, also improvements have been made in the Bakery Department, and a cooling room added - an undertaking which has been needed for some time past to provide for increasing trade - this work will, we hope, be completed shortly.

They wouldn't stay flat.
Barbara Large

It was not easy to photograph these plans. Before they had been sent to the Hampshire Record Office they had been folded away for years so they were stiff and just would not stay flat.

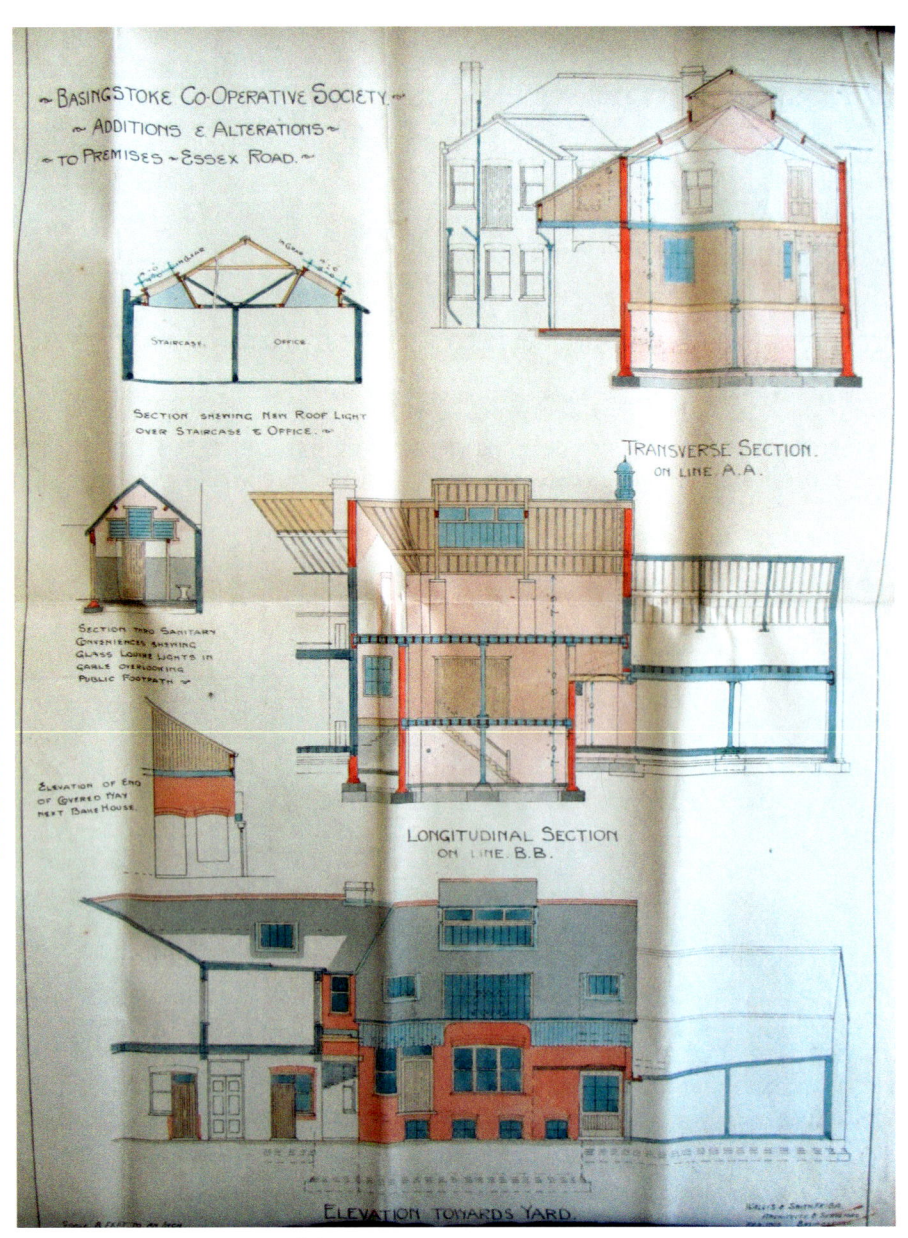

HRO 58M75/BP564

In order to avoid loss of time, as well as additional expense to the Society which must necessarily result from pressure of business on Friday and Saturday evenings, Members are earnestly requested to make their purchases as early in the week as possible, or to leave their orders at the Stores; forms can be had on application to the Manager. Carriage will be paid by the Society on all parcels of 5s. and upwards sent into the country by carriers or train, except in those villages where the Society's own van makes regular deliveries. In those places Members should send in their orders so that they reach the Stores the day previous to the day for delivery; if this is not done delivery cannot be guaranteed, and Members must pay their own carriage.

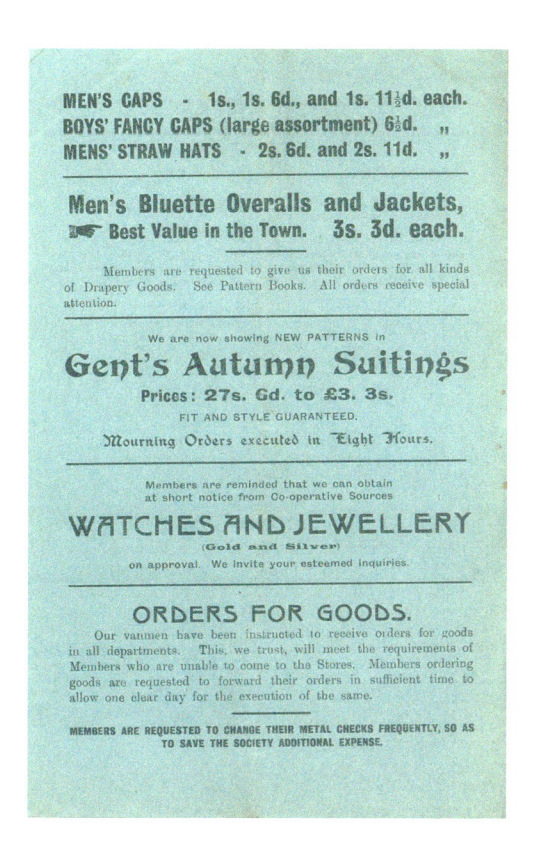

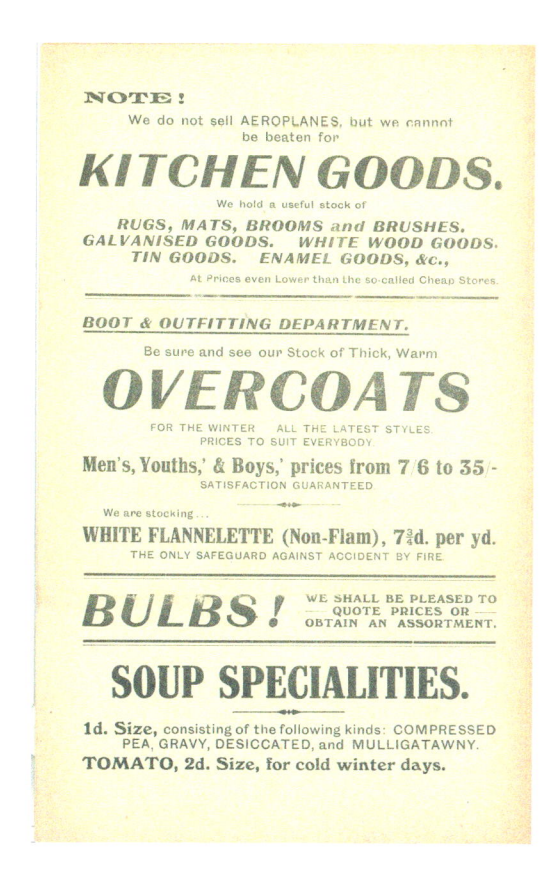

MEN'S CAPS - 1s., 1s. 6d., and 1s. 11½d. each.
BOYS' FANCY CAPS (large assortment) 6½d. „
MENS' STRAW HATS - 2s. 6d. and 2s. 11d. „

Men's Bluette Overalls and Jackets,
☞ Best Value in the Town. **3s. 3d. each.**

Members are requested to give us their orders for all kinds of Drapery Goods. See Pattern Books. All orders receive special attention.

We are now showing NEW PATTERNS in

Gent's Autumn Suitings
Prices: 27s. 6d. to £3. 3s.
FIT AND STYLE GUARANTEED.

Mourning Orders executed in Eight Hours.

Members are reminded that we can obtain at short notice from Co-operative Sources

WATCHES AND JEWELLERY
(Gold and Silver)
on approval. We invite your esteemed inquiries.

ORDERS FOR GOODS.
Our vanmen have been instructed to receive orders for goods in all departments. This, we trust, will meet the requirements of Members who are unable to come to the Stores. Members ordering goods are requested to forward their orders in sufficient time to allow one clear day for the execution of the same.

MEMBERS ARE REQUESTED TO CHANGE THEIR METAL CHECKS FREQUENTLY, SO AS TO SAVE THE SOCIETY ADDITIONAL EXPENSE.

NOTE!
We do not sell AEROPLANES, but we cannot be beaten for

KITCHEN GOODS.
We hold a useful stock of
RUGS, MATS, BROOMS and BRUSHES.
GALVANISED GOODS. WHITE WOOD GOODS.
TIN GOODS. ENAMEL GOODS, &c.,
At Prices even Lower than the so-called Cheap Stores.

BOOT & OUTFITTING DEPARTMENT.
Be sure and see our Stock of Thick, Warm

OVERCOATS
FOR THE WINTER   ALL THE LATEST STYLES.
PRICES TO SUIT EVERYBODY.

Men's, Youths,' & Boys,' prices from 7/6 to 35/-
SATISFACTION GUARANTEED.

We are stocking...
WHITE FLANNELETTE (Non-Flam), 7¾d. per yd.
THE ONLY SAFEGUARD AGAINST ACCIDENT BY FIRE.

BULBS! WE SHALL BE PLEASED TO QUOTE PRICES OR OBTAIN AN ASSORTMENT.

SOUP SPECIALITIES.
1d. Size, consisting of the following kinds: COMPRESSED PEA, GRAVY, DESICCATED, and MULLIGATAWNY.
TOMATO, 2d. Size, for cold winter days.

"EACH FOR ALL, AND ALL FOR EACH"
It has always been the aim of the Committee to study the wants and requirements of the
SOCIETY'S MANY MEMBERS.
Our newest provision is
A SHOP FRONT WINDOW,
specially decorated and made up to date, for the purpose of showing the variety and quality of our
CHOICE CAKES, PASTRY, &c.
Don't scatter the advantages of membership by buying elsewhere than at our own Shop.

C.W.S

SUMMER FESTIVAL
FLOWER SHOW
FOR YOUNG CO-OPERATORS.

Have you bought your Seeds yet? We want to see the finest blooms of your garden. To ensure this you must

BUY YOUR SEEDS AT ONCE AND AT THE STORES

The General Meeting on August 12th 1913 was held in the Coronation Hall (for a time this was the name for the Masonic Hall).

Children's Festivals

Children had a good time in 1907.

> BASINGSTOKE CO-OPERATIVE SOCIETY, LTD.-
> Annual festival, to-day (Saturday), in the Vicarage meadow, 2 p.m. Games, conjuring, ventriloquism, performing dog, juggler, etc. Tea and refreshments. The band of the North Hants Iron Works will lead the procession and play in the grounds. Admission free. The Stores will be closed at 12 noon. –Advt.

North Hants Iron Works Band

HCMS

A full report was printed in the *Hants & Berks Gazette* on 27th July.

The incidents of the day appealed most to the imagination of the children. The procession, formed of members' children, accompanied by the Band of the North Hants Iron Works and the Society's vehicles, marched through the most populous districts of the town—May Street, Alexandra Road, Flaxfield, into Church Street. The march occupied about forty minutes. The enthusiasm along the route was very marked. The children's tea (given free to members' children to the number of 778) took place about 4.30, and was keenly enjoyed; and there could be no possibility of any disquieting suggestions as to the health of the coming generation.

After tea bags of sweets and a piece of "Basingstoke Co-op Rock" was given to each child. Races, swings, a Punch and Judy show, a performing dog, ventriloquism and conjuring divided the remainder of the evening. Light refreshments were served from two marquees by a staff of ladies, whose wages for work well done was the pleasure of witnessing others' enjoyment. The National Anthem, played by the band, terminated the proceedings.

In 1913 the *Hants & Berks Gazette* reported that the twelfth children's festival had been held at Sherborne House, and the procession from the Wheatsheaf paddock was headed by the band of the Mechanics' Institute. The report stated that "It was probably the largest gathering that had ever assembled on a similar occasion."

Then the report continued, "About a thousand children sat down to tea in the open, and the adults partook of the refreshing beverage in a marquee. That co-operative appetites are hearty may be judged from the fact that a record was established in the quantity of provisions consumed, viz., 520lbs of cake, 92 4lb loaves, besides sponge rolls and jam sandwiches."

Sherborne House

There were prizes for an advertisement costume competition, races, skipping and threading the needle, as well as for flowers and vegetables. The Women's Guild organised a sale of needlework, with the proceeds going to the education fund. "An interesting display was given by the gymnastic and ambulance squad of the Baden-Powell Scouts, who also performed a musical drill and other exercises. A tournament on donkeys afforded considerable amusement." There was dancing to the music of the Mechanics' Band, followed by a half-hour concert in the flower show tent, "which had then been cleared and illuminated with fairy lights." Songs were sung, one with a cello obligato, followed by a cello solo.

Nothing seems to have been overlooked: "A Red Cross tent, with bed and all sorts of appliances for dealing with casualties, was on the ground, but the nurses on duty had nothing serious to deal with."

Finally it was announced that "Mr Hobbs took a number of photographs, copies of which can be obtained at his studio in Sarum Hill, Basingstoke".

THE WAR CHANGED PEOPLE'S LIVES

1914-1918

... War work at Thornycrofts and Wallis & Steevens ...

Winifred Griffiths wrote her autobiography **One Woman's Story** but it was not published until in 1975 when it appeared in the compilation **Useful Toil** edited by John Burnett (Penguin). We are grateful to her family for permission to include this extract, a unique account of working in Basingstoke's Co-op during the First World War.

Winifred was born in High Street, Overton on 21st May 1895, the second of four children. Her father, William George Rutley, worked at the local paper mill and was a Wesleyan lay preacher. Winifred went to the local National School, where she was top of her class in her final year and won the coveted 'guinea bible' but the family could not afford to keep her at school, so she left at the age of fourteen. She began a correspondence course to train for teaching but had to give up for lack of money to buy textbooks. So she began an apprenticeship at Burberry's (at 3s a week, plus 2s 6d for rail-travel), then worked for a ready-made tailoring firm (6s 2d for all the stitching in a lined suit jacket). When that firm closed down she went into domestic service as a housemaid for Dr & Mrs Scott at East Oakley House.

In May 1914 I had my nineteenth birthday. I had spent three years at East Oakley House and life still went on in a fairly pleasant way. One day I was glancing through a magazine which had been left around the house when I chanced to read a short article by an economist which I shall always remember. It caused a profound change in my thinking about life. I had never met a socialist and yet this short article was to make a socialist of me. The article gave as the author's opinion that the world should and could be organized so that every able-bodied person did a fair share of useful work and that everybody - children, the aged and the disabled included - should have a fair share of the necessities of life and of the results of human labour. In other words the rule should be "From each according to his ability, and to each according to his need." The writer also gave as his opinion that a great many people worked very hard at tasks that were unnecessary and did not contribute to the common good, instancing those who worked to provide luxuries for the rich, while the poor were in dire need.

Then the War started and it was changing people's lives. There was a great deal of talk about "jobs of national importance" for women as well as men. Surely soon my chance would come. One day Mrs Scott spoke to me, letting me know that she knew how I was feeling. She told me that the manager of the Co-operative Stores in Basingstoke was on the look-out for young women to train to take the places of grocery assistants who were joining the Forces. She was prepared to give me a very good reference if I would like to apply. I accepted her offer with alacrity and in due course was taken on in the grocery department of the Co-operative Stores

I found on my arrival at the Co-op that I was not expected to serve in the shop right away but was to have some time to get used to the variety of goods and the prices. During this period I worked in what was called "Dispatch". This was a room behind the shop in which orders were put up. In charge of this room was a little man with a fair moustache. He was not at all formidable as a "boss", but was quiet and firm and slightly humorous and organized the work very well. The first job I was put to do was weighing sugar. Sacks of sugar were stored in a loft over Dispatch. This sugar was tipped down a chute to a bench below. It was my job to stand all day by this bench opening bags, filling sugar into them with a scoop and weighing them in one, two, three and four pounds. As a variation I sometimes switched over to lump sugar and when sufficient sugar had been done, soda was sent down the chute. Soda was a commodity bought by most housewives before the advent of soap powders.

After a few days at this rather monotonous task I was allowed to help with putting up orders. A very large number of these orders were from country customers. These orders were collected in late afternoon by the carriers who plied between villages and town.

Friday evening was a busy time in the shop, as many members came then to collect groceries and to pay bills. As bad luck would have it, I was sent down for the first time to help on the grocery counter on a Friday evening. I was so bewildered that I am afraid I made a fine mess of things. I had to take payment of bills and the method of receipting had not been explained to me. When trying to serve customers I did not know where things were kept, nor yet had I memorized all the prices. I had not acquired the knack of making tidy packets for goods like dried fruit, rice and tapioca, and numerous others which were kept loose in drawers and had to be weighed as needed. To crown all, most customers expected their goods to be done up in a large paper parcel. It seems now at this time, when all goods are packeted, and self-service is the order of the day, almost incredible the amount of work involved in serving just one customer under the old conditions.

We sold some goods for which there was no room in the shop, such things as potatoes, corn for chickens, barley meal, bran and other animal feeding-stuffs which had to be measured in pint, quart or gallon measures and packed in paper bags. Another article was common salt, which came to the shop in long thick bars, from which we had to cut a thick slice to be sold for 1½d. Yet another commodity was a long bar of household soap which might be bought whole or in halves or quarters and, for a change from solids, there was draught vinegar, to be drawn off into a measure and transferred to the customer's own bottle or jug. All these goods and others too were stored in rooms behind the shop and had to be fetched and weighed or measured as needed.

The shop assistant's job was not a light one in those days, neither was it a clean one. So many things to weigh and so much to fetch and carry played havoc with our hands and with our overalls. We had a little retreat where we could wash our hands, in cold water, but too many trips to "Scarborough", as it came to be called, were apt to be frowned upon. So we just wiped our hands on our overalls - and that was that! I soon learned to be wary of "Committee men" who sometimes appeared without warning, and were suspected by the employees of "snooping".

At the back of the grocery premises was a baker's, where not only bread but confectionery was made. One of our shop windows was given over to a display of cakes which could be bought at the provision counter. In course of time I was given the job of dressing this window and I found it a pleasant interlude.

Just after I was taken on at the Co-op, two other women also made a start. Both had come long distances, one from Somerset and the other from Yorkshire. Jennie, the Yorkshire lass, was soon the life and soul of the place. In no time she became, without doubt, the most popular member of staff. She was good-looking, vivacious, cheerful and kind. Obviously life was a great adventure: exciting things were always happening. Life's little incidents took on a magical quality when Jennie recounted them. No one could be cross or gloomy when she was around. I was thrilled when she asked me to come out with her to an evening class, or to the cinema on our half-day, or to church or a walk on Sunday. The Co-op had found "digs" for her but the food was in short supply and soon she was looking for another place to stay. An elderly woman, who lived just opposite the shop, offered her a room. She found on going to visit Mrs Diddums that there was really place for two, and that two sharing would pay less. Jennie asked me if I would like to join her. We would share a room and have all our meals provided for 10s a week each, on condition that we gave a hand with the housework. So we clinched the deal and moved in.

At the shop we were always busy, for there never seemed to be a complete staff. Men left to join up and as yet the management could not imagine they could get along with women only. In years prior to the war, recruits to the grocery and provision trade had been required to serve several years' apprenticeship and afterwards a long period as ordinary assistants before they could become "first hand", that is, to be in charge of either the grocery or provision counter. Hence the Co-op tried whenever possible to replace the men who left for the army by other men. One day there appeared a young Welshman, who obviously knew his job very well, although this was the first post he had ever taken outside his native Wales. He was a pleasant bright-eyed little fellow in his early twenties, who soon became popular with the staff. I discovered in conversation with him that he had his serious side and he had thought quite deeply about life and that he was a socialist. I was quite thrilled to meet a real live socialist, for I had known, in a sense, that I was one ever since I read the economist's article that had so affected me when I was at East Oakley. Now I was to be persuaded of wider implications of socialist thought. Up until now I had been a loyal supporter of the war effort, only wishing I could play a more useful part in helping the country. But now under the influence of this young Welshman, I was to revise my ideas. He contended that the ghastly war was the outcome of the capitalist system and that socialists ought to resist it.

Of course it took time for me to be wholly convinced, but Edgar lent me books and pamphlets to read, and gradually I came round to thinking he was right.

Edgar soon joined the crowd of us from the shop who went together to the cinema on Thursday evenings and sometimes on other little outings. The Women's Co-operative Guild was very good to the staff in arranging little farewell parties for the boys who left to join the Army. Daisy, the girl from Somerset, was in digs with a girl called Dolly, who worked in a rather high-class grocery store in town. She would bring Dolly along with her to our outings. In this way Edgar met Dolly and they became very friendly and soon they were as good as engaged.

Looking back, it seems as if we were all there together for a long time, but in reality it was only a very short period. Change was in the air, first one left, then another. Conscription was now in force and all the youngsters had to go in turn. Edgar had his calling-up papers and had to go back to Wales. He had at first some thoughts of resistance as a so-called C.O. [Conscientious Objector] but it did not come off. I think Dolly had not developed any understanding of that point of view, and her attitude was probably the deciding factor. Anyhow, he joined the Army.

Meanwhile in the shop still more changes. Suddenly we heard the manager was leaving, not for the Army or anything like that, but to take on a business of his own in a little town some few miles away. Worse was to come. He persuaded Jennie and Daisy to leave and to take jobs with him at his new shop. This to me was a great shock. To lose Jennie was to lose the last bit of sunshine from our little circle. I really felt quite dejected.

Then one day I was surprised to receive a letter and a parcel of books from Wales, from a young man who it appeared was a close friend of Edgar. This young man was a miner and an active socialist and he signed himself "Yours in the cause, J. Griffiths".

Thus through the pages of a letter and the loan of some books I met the man who was to be my husband. From then onward we corresponded regularly, expressing in our letters our ideas and ideals about the world and its problems. It seemed that we had a good deal in common. Later in the year Dolly had an invitation to come down to Wales when Edgar had leave from the Army, and I received an invitation from J. Griffiths to come down with her and meet the socialist group to which both he and Edgar belonged.

We paid a visit to the socialist club - The White House - and met the comrades there. I was thrilled and thought I was getting near to the heart of things that mattered. Near the end of our visit, after Edgar had returned to the Army, Jim and I came to an understanding as to how we felt towards each other. From then on we considered it an engagement, though it was not formalized with a ring - as we did not believe in such conventional arrangements!

And so, for Dolly and me, an end to our holiday adventure in Wales, and a return to work. I become a "hand" on provisions but for me there was no longer much joy in work. Almost all the staff from the manager down had changed, and I came to the conclusion I also would seek a change. There was a grocery and provision business in town called Walkers Stores which was advertising for a girl to learn the work of the provision counter. I applied and got the job.

Shop assistants at Walkers: Winifred is in the lower row on the far left

Photos courtesy of Harold & David Griffiths

Although she was soon promoted to "first hand" at Walkers, Winifred moved to Llanelli to be close to Jim and worked in the Co-operative store there till they were married in 1918. When Jim attended the Central Labour College in London she worked to support them both. In 1934 Jim became President of the South Wales Miners' Federation. Two years later he was elected Labour MP for Llanelli. In the Labour Government in 1945 he became Minister of National Insurance and later Secretary of State for Wales.

Winifred herself spoke on women's rights and became chairman of the local women's section of the Labour Party, district councillor, member of the board of guardians and local magistrate. During the Second World War she joined the Women's Voluntary Service and was involved in social work. She stood unsuccessfully as a candidate for the London County Council, was governor of two secondary schools and on committees for old people's homes and children's homes, becoming a JP in 1951. Jim died in 1975 and Winifred in 1982.

At the start of the First World War, a Co-op committee meeting noted that . . .

"It is unfortunate that employees joining up do not inform us instead of merely not turning up.

Co-operative members were asked to 'make allowances when doing their shopping as we have had to replace men by women'.

HCMS P2003.400.428

This horse-drawn Co-op delivery cart with a woman driver had come from the Co-op stables in Essex Road and was standing in Penrith Road. The house with bay windows later had a prominent role in the activities of the Co-operative Women's Guild (see page 104).

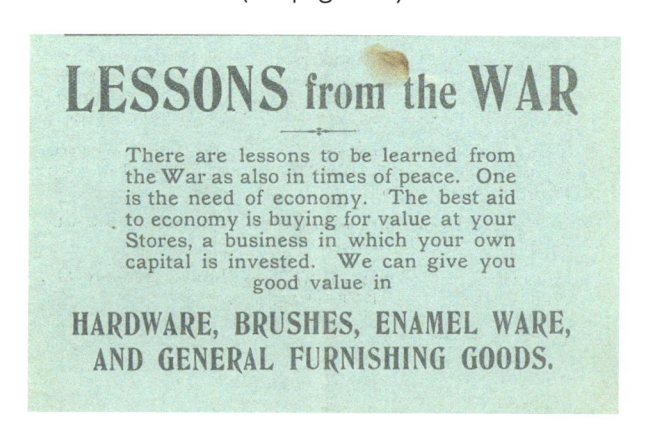

LESSONS from the WAR

There are lessons to be learned from the War as also in times of peace. One is the need of economy. The best aid to economy is buying for value at your Stores, a business in which your own capital is invested. We can give you good value in

HARDWARE, BRUSHES, ENAMEL WARE, AND GENERAL FURNISHING GOODS.

Overton

On 9th October 1916 it was reported that Mr Ratley of Overton had asked if the Committee "could arrange a means to educate the people of Overton to the advantage of co-operation and if possible find means to supply the members by running a van to Overton."

The effects of war

The following particulars as to the present position of the society will be of interest to the general public. The members number 1303, which compared with 1151 last year shows an increase of 152. The profits paid out as dividend for the quarter ended June 2, 1915, amounted to £992. The sales for the half year ended June 2 amounted to £22,270, which compared with £13,709 shows an increase of no less than £8,561. Part of this, it will be noted, was due to the presence of troops and to the increased prices. The share capital of members this year amounts to £10,587, an increase of £1927 compared with last year. Mr. Ellingham, the society's Manager, writes: -

When the history of the European War comes to be written no co-operator will have cause to be ashamed of Co-operation, but will have reason to be proud of what the movement has been able to do. The Co-operative Wholesale Society, the *communis mater* of the affiliated English Co-operative Societies, representing about three million working men and women, has through the C.W.S. Bank taken up War Loan to the extent of £1,400,000. The Basingstoke Society has invested in the Wholesale Society £3,291, the savings of its members. This amount is small perhaps, but is sufficient to indicate the strength and financial solidarity of the Society. If an average of £5 per member were invested in War Loan by the members of this Society, it would represent no less a sum than £6,515. While indirectly we have thus subscribed to the building of the great War Loan, we are in addition paying 5 per cent, on £10,587 members' invested capital.

Mr Ellingham explained how prices had been affected by war.

The war has shown that co-operation can modify prices in the interests of the people. We have reason to know that the members of the Basingstoke Society are grateful and satisfied that the essentials of co-operation have been exhibited and practised by deliberate and yet not philanthropic action in maintaining the price of food at reasonable rates. This policy is not vindictive; it is co-operative. The consumer was protected from having to submit to the prices fixed by syndicates and other concerns out of proportion to the actual value and cost of daily necessities. Thus the Government was given the precedent for its recent action in fixing some maximum prices. In the early days of the war crisis in 1914 it was difficult to renew stocks of goods at prices ruling before the war, and in some cases marketable articles were enhanced to more than double their previous figures. This Society was for some two months enabled to give its customers the advantage of considerable stocks at normal prices. Take three articles of food only - rice, sugar and butter; no less a sum than £482.10s.8d could have been netted for profits if we had advanced prices in sympathy with competition. From time to time the Board of Trade issue a scale of comparative prices, and it was noted that the Co-operative Society for a long period maintained a price for bread to its customers which was lower than the general prices current. This applies also to coal. In the House of Commons on Monday, March 15th, 1915, Mr. B. Peto asked whether the Government were giving any financial or other assistance to the Co-operative Wholesale or any other Society which would enable them to undersell traders who had to buy flour, sugar or other food-stuffs in the open market. The Government's reply to Mr. Peto was—No, sir.

The Basingstoke Co-operative Society has now been established 22 years and has amply demonstrated the broad mission of co-operation to the wage-earning classes, namely, that the good things of life should be more freely and fully enjoyed by those who create them.

HBG 7.8.1915

That year, also, "owing to the war the usual indoor gathering of the members had been dispensed with", but the Committee decided to allow tea and some games for the children. So, "Mr Horry, the proprietor of the Wheatsheaf Hotel, granted the use of the Wheatsheaf paddock for the marshalling of the procession, and starting from this point, and headed by the Borough Band, the procession had a short march to Brambly Meadow, which they entered from Winchester Road."

There were refreshments, of course. "Between eleven and twelve hundred mouths, mostly young ones, were satisfied with a bountiful tea in the open air, after tea each child was presented with a bag of wholesome sweets and during the evening refreshments were served from a marquee." There were separate sports for boys and girls, for small amounts of cash: flat races and striking the peg. The band continued to play "and the festival, which was favoured with dry weather, passed off very happily."

In 1916 the Children's Festival was held in a different place.

> £1.1.0 was given to the West Ham Red Cross Hospital and it was agreed that the wounded soldiers be invited to the Children's Festival at Goldings Park.

Problems of staffing were noted. At the General meeting on July 10th it was reported that "a letter had been received from the Auditor pointing out that owing to the shortage of staff caused by the war he was unable to continue the Stock taking till after the War. The Chairman stated that the Committee undertook to take the Stock and that there were Expenses to pay owing to some of them losing time from their employment - agreed to pay the Committee for taking the stock."

It was probably staffing problems that led to the next notice.

To the Members of the Basingstoke Co=operative Society Limited.

In accordance with the Resolution passed at the last Quarterly Meeting,

"on and after Monday, November 29th, 1915, all Bread, Flour, "and Cakes must be paid for on delivery, or a token or tokens "given in exchange, previously purchased at the Stores for Cash,"

the Committee appeal to the Members to give them all possible assistance which will save time and clerical work to our mutual advantage.

Will Members in the town please apply at the Store for one week's supply of tokens, to be paid for at the time (for which they will receive a Dividend Check), and give them up to the Roundsman in exchange for Bread, Flour, &c., as they require. Should they run out of tokens they may pay cash, in which case the Roundsman will give Dividend Check as usual.

Country Members who may find it inconvenient to attend the Store personally may order a supply from the Roundsman, who will bring them in a sealed packet, with Dividend Checks, on his next visit. Each packet must be paid for on delivery.

Members who may happen to be out from home when the Roundsman calls, should previously arrange with him where to leave the Bread, &c., required,—always leaving the necessary token or tokens in exchange.

On behalf of the Committee,

Yours faithfully,

J. TYLER, *Secretary*.

In October it was announced that the Drapery Department was now opened and was doing very well. It was listed in a quarterly report the next month.

Quarter ending 28th November 1916

This Society supplies Boots and shoes, Drapery, Men's and Boys' clothing, and Umbrellas; Bedsteads, bedding, Carpets and Furniture; Sewing and Wringing Machines; Clocks, Watches, Bicycles, Pianos, Books, &c., from the Co-operative Wholesale Society, of which our Society is a member.

The same report carried a historic notice:

> Married or single women may become Members in their own right, and have the same power as other members.

Winifred Griffiths would have been pleased with the Society's empowerment of women at a time when they hadn't yet got the vote.

Women were making themselves heard because in April Mrs Greenaway had asked if an Educational Committee could be formed. However, the Chairman said it had been decided some years ago to make the General Committee responsible for the working of the Educational Fund so she didn't get her way.

Winifred Griffiths' involvement with the aims of the Co-operative Movement developed alongside her growing interest in the Labour Party. In 1917 a motion was put to a Basingstoke General Meeting to donate £5 to the divisional Labour Party "believing it is essential that the whole of the working class movement should combine to oppose the capitalistic forces" - no doubt she would have supported that but the resolution was lost.

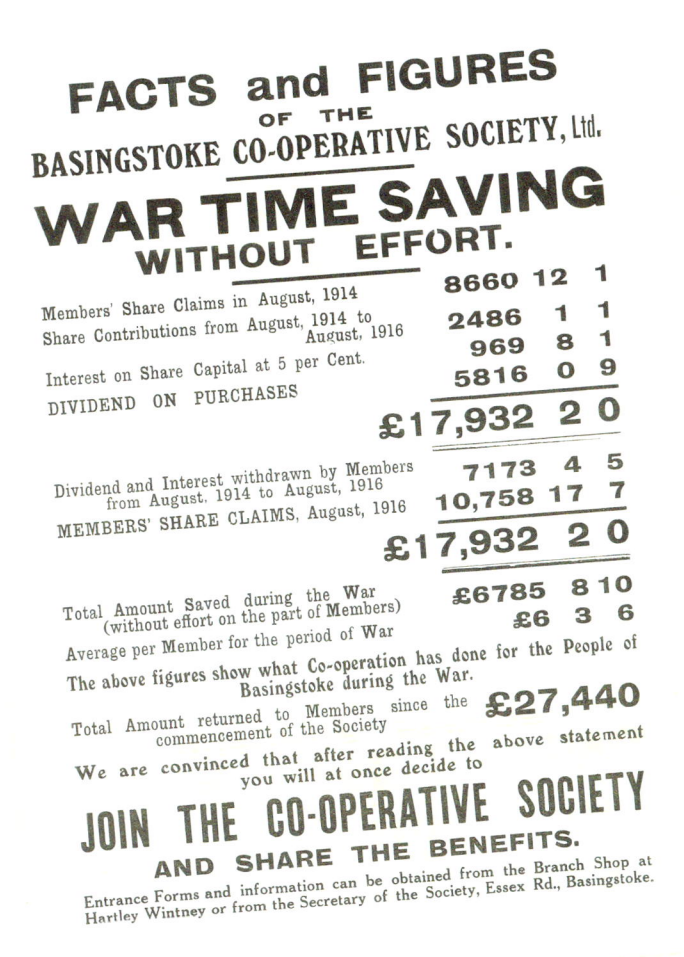

FACTS and FIGURES OF THE BASINGSTOKE CO-OPERATIVE SOCIETY, Ltd.

WAR TIME SAVING WITHOUT EFFORT.

	£ s d
Members' Share Claims in August, 1914	8660 12 1
Share Contributions from August, 1914 to August, 1916	2486 1 1
Interest on Share Capital at 5 per Cent.	969 8 1
DIVIDEND ON PURCHASES	5816 0 9
	£17,932 2 0
Dividend and Interest withdrawn by Members from August, 1914 to August, 1916	7173 4 5
MEMBERS' SHARE CLAIMS, August, 1916	10,758 17 7
	£17,932 2 0
Total Amount Saved during the War (without effort on the part of Members)	£6785 8 10
Average per Member for the period of War	£6 3 6

The above figures show what Co-operation has done for the People of Basingstoke during the War.

Total Amount returned to Members since the commencement of the Society **£27,440**

We are convinced that after reading the above statement you will at once decide to

JOIN THE CO-OPERATIVE SOCIETY AND SHARE THE BENEFITS.

Entrance Forms and information can be obtained from the Branch Shop at Hartley Wintney or from the Secretary of the Society, Essex Rd., Basingstoke.

Hartley Wintney

Despite the problems of war-time, the Basingstoke Co-operative Society was able to open its No. 1 branch in the High Street, Hartley Wintney. By January 1917 it had 137 members, with a trade of £490 10 3.

> **Quarter ended June 4th, 1917**
>
> **Agenda** Resolutions - Moved by R. Howard, Seconded by F. Tomkins:
> 1   That this meeting decides to make an allowance (in kind) to Mrs. Fulbrook as a mark of appreciation by the society of an old employee.
> 2   That in order to give effect to previous resolution we decide that Mrs. Fulbrook shall be supplied (free of cost) weekly with four loaves, 2 lbs of sugar, 1 lb Butter, ½ cwt. coal."

In October that year "alterations were being proceeded with at the Stores and included the enlargement of the Grocery Shop and the installation of a drawplate Oven and Electric Hoist". There were problems with the irregularity of food supplies.

In January 1918, in the 102nd Report and Balance sheet the Committee announced that they hoped in the near future to receive the support of the members on cash trading.

> Trade expenses included: £   s   d
>   Rent of Wharf   1. 10. 0.
>   Stable & rolling Stock   9. 17. 1.
>   Shoeing & Veterinary   36 . 9 . 7.
>   Fodder & meadow   24. 16. 0.
>   Horse hire   16. 0.
>
> Assets included: Horse £49
> Cash expenses included £1. 2. 0. Manure

Peace at last!

This was the first Co-op advertisement to appear in the *Hants & Berks Gazette* since 1914.

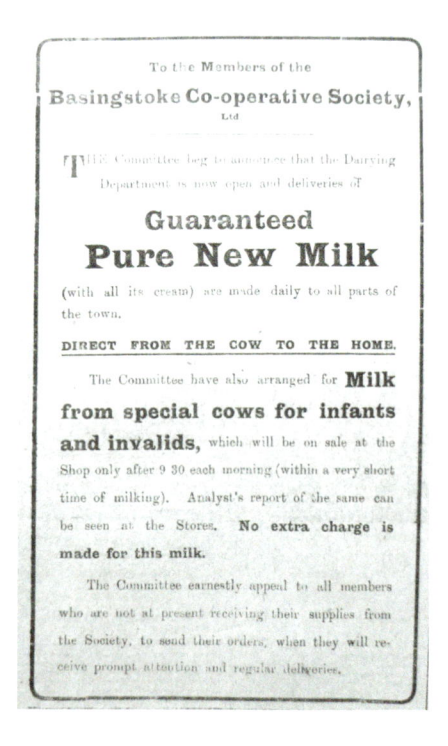

"Peace Day" 19.7.19.

In July the usual outing was postponed because of the Peace celebrations but the children's festival was held at Sherborne House.

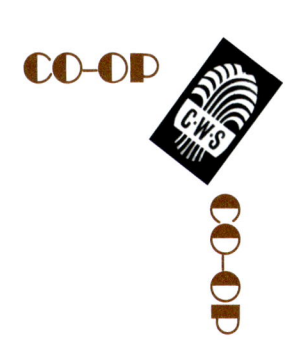

BETWEEN THE WARS

1919 and the Twenties

... Population 12,723 (1921) ... Venture bus company set up (1925) ...

Essex Road

Minute books of the Basingstoke Co-operative Society in 1919 reported the purchase of property adjoining the stores in Essex Road, the removal of the stable (which was replaced by a van shed) and the extension of the stores. This would now include a new butcher's shop and cold storage, provision for dairying and the confectionery department and an extension of the Secretary's office on the ground floor, with workrooms upstairs for dress-making and millinery outfitting; the former boot shop being transferred upstairs and the space used for milk and confectionery. The architects were again Wallis & Smith.

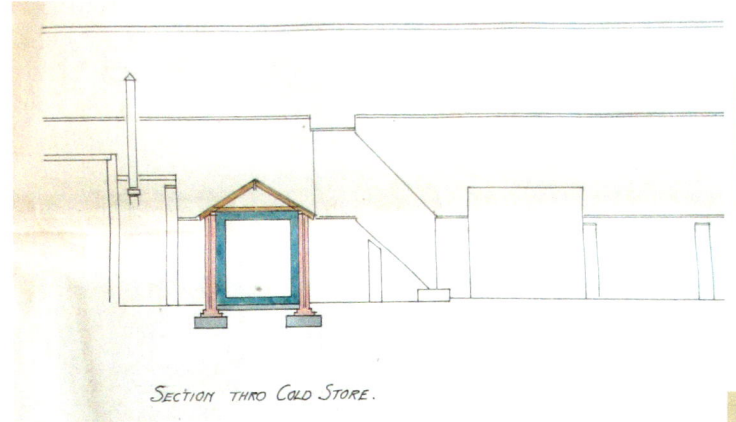

HRO 58M74/BP738

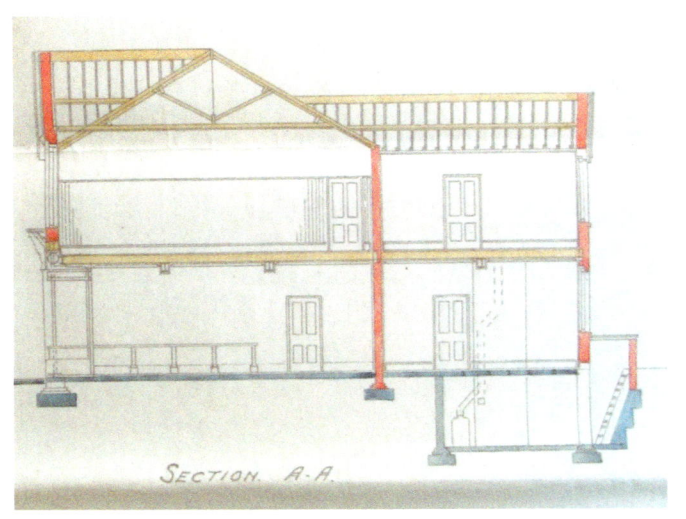

BWM 2007.75

This photograph shows employees of the Basingstoke Co-operative Society Ltd outside the despatch department of the Co-op in Essex Road, in an area between the bakery (off the photo to the left) and the bottling plant (off the photo to the right). The man in a white overall, 5th from the left on the back row, is Mr Stannard who later became manager of the Co-op in New Street. The man 7th from the left on the back row is Mr Herbert Toop (see page 47). The two boys in frilled white aprons in the foreground are provision hands who divided dairy goods like butter supplied in wholesale portions into domestic-sized portion for home use. This photograph was taken about 1921-22; all information was supplied by Mr Toop's son, Ken (see page 61).

In 1923 the Committee reported at the General Meeting that the stables belonging to the Essex Road premises had been found to be very dilapidated (it looks as if that part of the 1919 plans had not been carried out) so it was decided to erect new brick stables on the far end of the vacant land at the back of the existing stables. Unfortunately there was no room to put in a lift to the drapery, boots and outfitting departments.

In April 1925 the Society sought planning permission for taking down the old building in Essex Road and erecting a new bakery and front shop to the north of the existing butchery department.

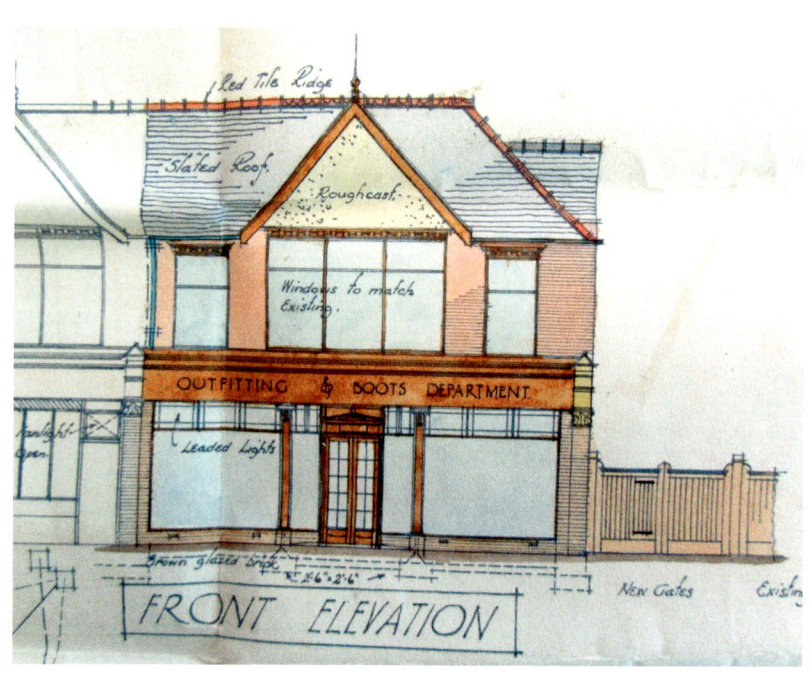

HRO 58M74/BP1035

The opening of the new premises in Essex Road was reported in the *Hants & Berks Gazette* on 1st May 1926. They were designed by Mr L G Ekins, head of the Architects Dept CWS, but his assistant, Mr Read, had direct control of this work. The builder was Mr H Goodall, charging £4,409 - Mr Ekins said he was almost a definition of a freak, an honest builder. Shop fittings in the outfitting and boots dept were supplied by Messrs Parnell & Son of Bristol for £720.

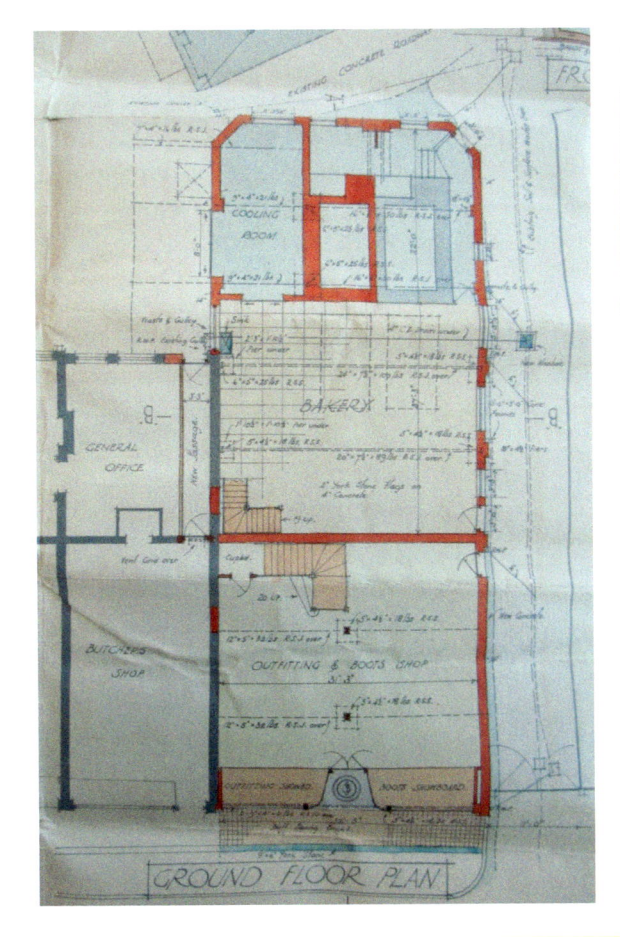

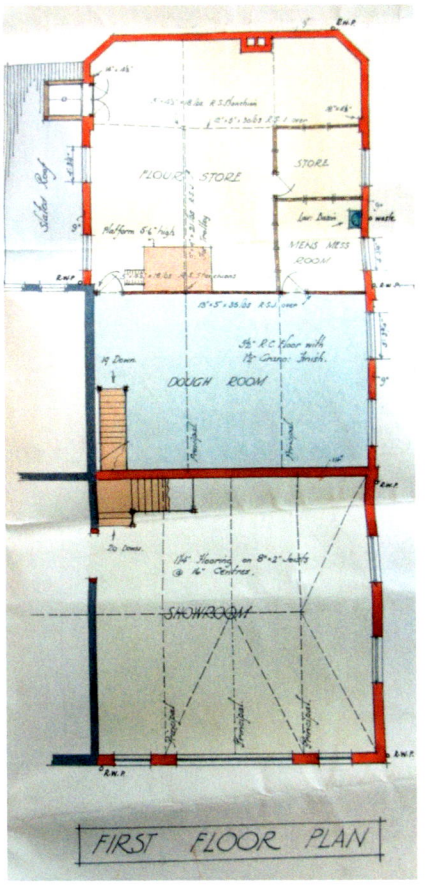

The new buildings have been erected where the workshop of the late Mr. Mundy, builder, formerly stood. They comprise a new bakery (the old one being now converted into a grocery warehouse) and abutting on the street are the new shop fronts of the boots and outfitting departments, over which are commodious and well equipped showrooms for the drapery and millinery departments. The alterations have made it possible for the society to develop the furniture and hardware business.

The architectural structure of the new bakery is almost square with numerous windows lying nearly flush with the walls. Within there is light and air in every department. The wall surface is faced with white glazed bricks and liberal coatings of white enamel on the woodwork give it an appearance of scrupulous cleanliness. The building is well ventilated and lighted. Access to the upper storey is provided by a staircase. So much for a glimpse of the exterior and interior, but there are much more important features to explain. Take for example the flour storage, situated on the top storey. It is the first link in the chain between raw flour and appetising bread. The flour is pulled up by an electric hoist and stored in level rows on a heavy solid floor, which supports 500 bags of flour, but the period of rest allowed is of short duration owing to the large trade. Flour is placed on a large platform by a mechanical pulley. From there it is put into a hopper and it is brushed through a fine sieve by an eccentric brush into a dough machine situated in the dough room. This latter is a long commodious apartment, covered with white glazed tiles, well ventilated, and lighted. There is a roof light in addition to windows, and electric light, also heat radiators and hot-water piping, these maintaining the proper temperature for maturing the doughs. On one side stands a dough mixer driven by a separate motor. In the space of a few minutes 280lbs of flour, salt, yeast, improver and water of the desired temperature from the tempering tank are thoroughly mixed, and the whole mass ejected into a trough placed near the machine. When all the troughs are full and put into their respective order, they are allowed to lie for the correct time for maturing; in reality subtly changed by a very simple form of cell life set up by yeast and water at a temperature of 74 degrees (Fahrenheit). On the ground floor below the dough room is the oven room, in which manufacture is completed. There is a chute from the dough room where the dough comes down to feed a divider, which has been installed by Messrs. Baker, Perkins, Ltd., Peterborough. Mechanical plungers and cylinders, together with dividing arrangements, split the dough into equal pieces of weight sufficient to meet the requirements of the law. The pieces of dough travel on a coned belt to an umbrella topped moulder, to be shaped round. They are then placed into drawers in a very large proving table and allowed to prove 16 minutes. After moulding all kinds of shaped loaves they are put on setters and transferred on four drawplate ovens each holding 180 loaves. After 45 minutes baking each plate in turn is pulled out, the bread placed on racks and taken to the loading room for cooling. Next, there is an electric three-speed cake machine, which can beat up any kind of cake. Near by stands a large confectionery table, where all the decorating and artistic sugar-work is done, also a prover full of steam proving buns, dough and lard cakes. The drawplate ovens are heated by hundreds of tubes fired by coke at the very back of the buildings, so that no dust can get into the main baking department. Everything has been done to ensure hygienic methods of the production of bread and confectionery. The members found the inspection of the new bakery interesting and instructive.

Not less so was their inspection of the dairy plant. The supplies of milk are brought from the farmer, every farmer from whom supplies are obtained being a member. The milk is put into the tank (or bath) from which it is pumped over the generative heater and flows on the inside of the machine. The hot milk passing through the inside brings the cold milk flowing over the outside of the machine to its proper temperature for cleaning purposes in the clarifier. The chief part in the clarifier is the bowl. This contains 33 small discs, which collect all the dirt, etc. from the milk. Passing on from the generative heater it goes to the cooler, the top portion of which is cooled by water, the lower by brine, and brought down to a temperature of 20 degrees. The plant is capable of dealing with 180 galls. per hour.

HBG 1.5.1926

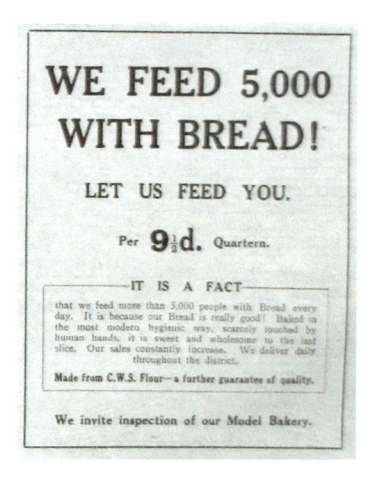

WE FEED 5,000 WITH BREAD!

LET US FEED YOU.

Per **9½d.** Quartern.

—IT IS A FACT—

that we feed more than 5,000 people with Bread every day. It is because our Bread is really good! Baked in the most modern hygienic way, scarcely touched by human hands, it is sweet and wholesome to the last slice. Our sales constantly increase. We deliver daily throughout the district.

Made from C.W.S. Flour—a further guarantee of quality.

We invite inspection of our Model Bakery.

During speeches at the opening ceremony, it was commented that "some people had remarked that it was difficult for a stranger to find the Stores, but although they were not in the shopping centre, they were fairly central as regards the lay-out of the town. They opened a branch in the main street about two years ago, and they hoped shortly to have an even more up-to-date shop there. They had recently purchased some premises. . . it would be only for grocery at first but there would be room upstairs for a catering business."

... *a small wooden cup* ...
Arthur Attwood

My mother had been issued with one of the early share numbers, number 70. Week after week I used to visit the Co-op Store at Essex Road, where the great fascination was to see the overhead system whereby money for customers' purchases was put in a small wooden cup and fitted to a holder which would be propelled by a spring along the overhead wires to the cashier's desk.

Moving into New Street

The desire to move to a more central position was no idle wish and New Street (once called Stew Lane, which may indicate a disreputable past) was now respectable and contained the Mechanics' Institute and Library.

Plans were submitted for branch premises at 17 New Street (HRO 58M74/BP3316). They were amended in July (HRO 58M74/BP1178) and approved, the new building being opened in 1927. This time the architect, Mr Ekins, used a very decorative Art Nouveau style of heading

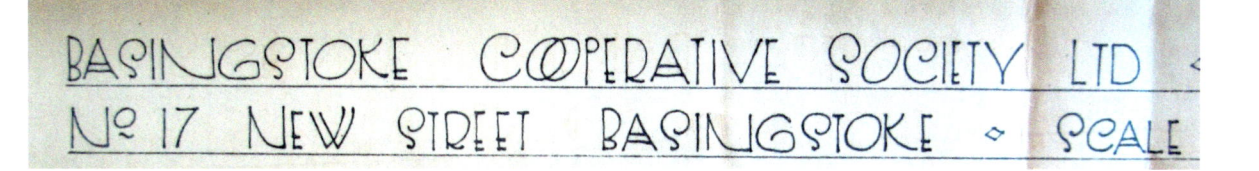

BASINGSTOKE COOPERATIVE SOCIETY LTD
No 17 NEW STREET BASINGSTOKE • SCALE

The grocery and confectionery shop stands on a site formerly occupied by the late Mr. F. P. Wyeth's boot and shoe shop. Mr. L. G. Ekins, architect to the Co-operative Wholesale Society, was responsible for the design, and he was assisted by Mr. W. J. Reed. The shop front is in mahogany, the contours being faced with St Anne marble, with Roman stone panels. The interior is 32 ft by 26 ft 8 ins. The rubber floor with marbled effect is laid on concrete. The walls are faced with white opal plate sub-divided with panels by means of black marmorite. The wall fixtures are chiefly carried out in marble, the cases being of mahogany. Stone steps at the back of the shop lead to a yard which communicates with the premises that are to be converted into a furnishing department. The builders were Messrs. Mussellwhite & Son; the fixtures were supplied by Messrs Parnell & Sons of Fishponds, Bristol, and the electric light installation was carried out by Mr E C Ford, Basingstoke.

HBG 23.7.1927

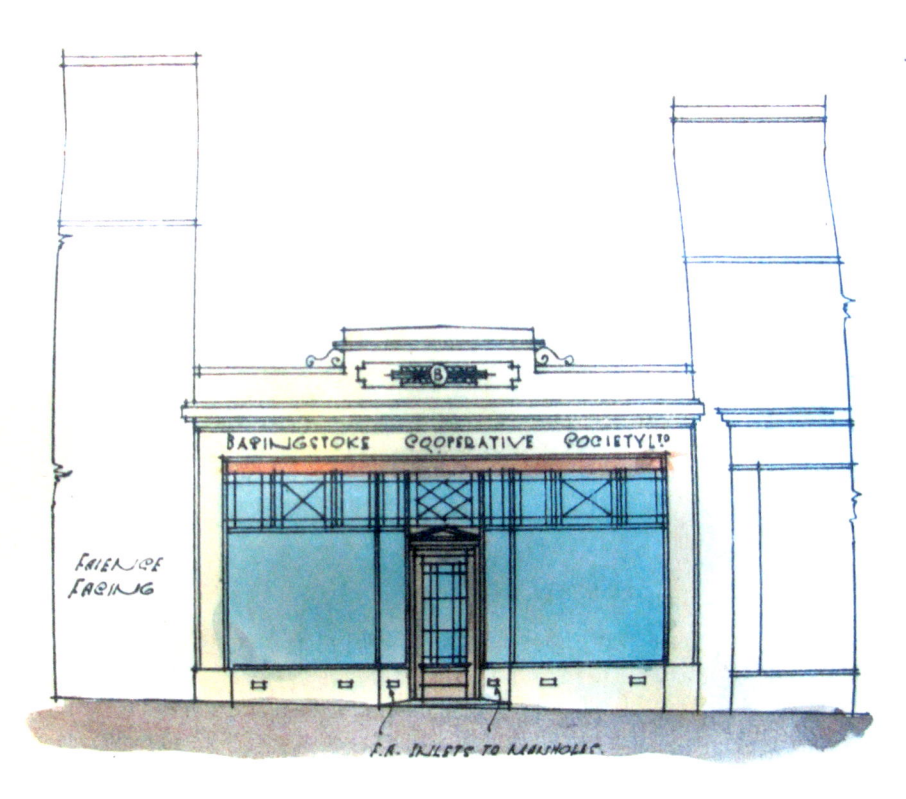

FRONT ELEVATION

HRO 58M74/BP1178

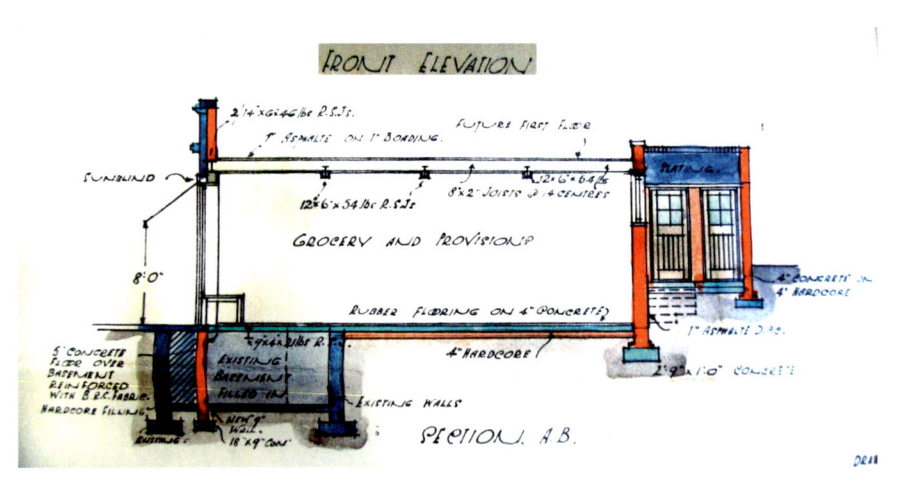

The decorative lettering is even used for the detailed captions, particularly the capital "S".

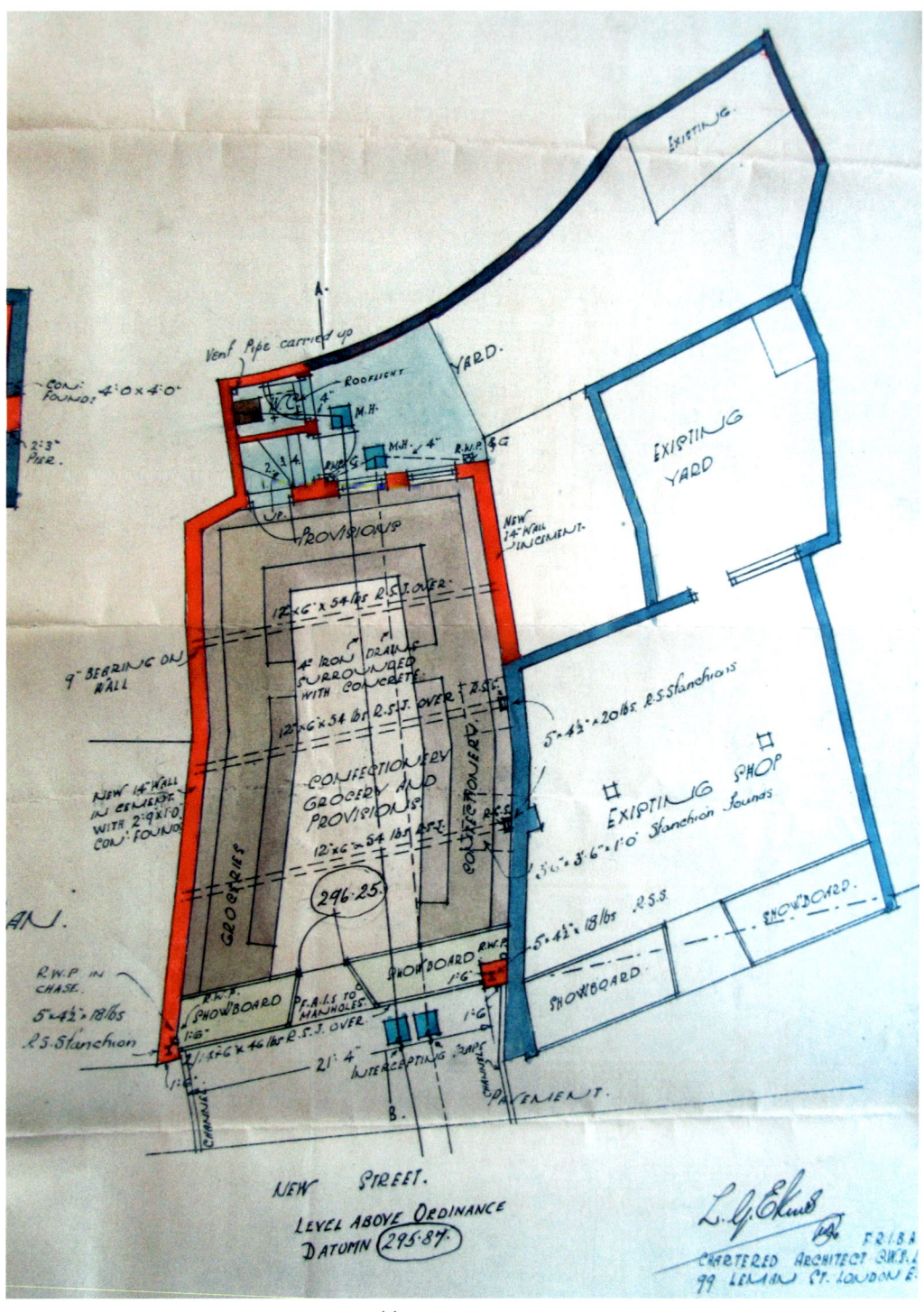

The National Co-operative Propaganda Campaign

You too could be a grateful customer (dressed in the latest fashions), meeting a friendly shop assistant You too could get money back from the Co-operative Stores but not from other shops.

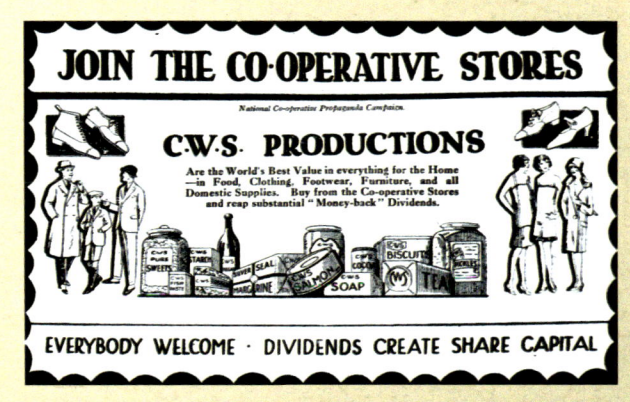

Advertisements

Now the Co-op were changing their policy on advertising, showing particular items. They even had a series of soap adverts for three successive weeks in June 1927. The CWS brand was prominent.

The Co-op countered the International Meat Company's claim with their own prices but they were beaten on all prices except sirloin.

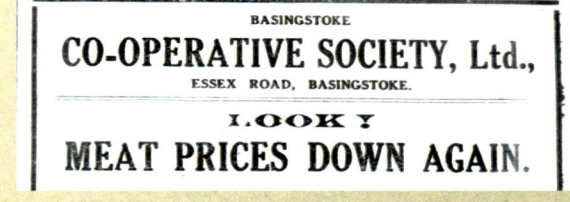

Even after expansion into New Street, Essex Road remained the Co-op headquarters.

Here is an early example of the "free offer".

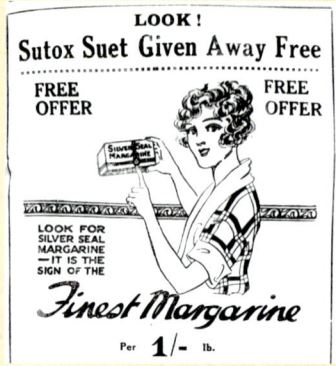

Advertisements illustrated the desirable attributes of modern life for women ...

and men ...

and for the family.

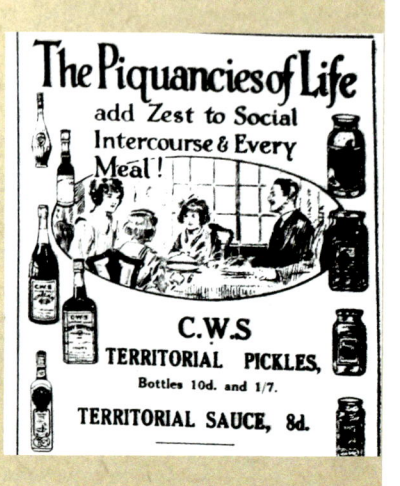

Deliveries

Country routes in winter...
Ken Toop

My father, Bert, was a Co-op delivery man in the early 1920s. The country people couldn't come in to the Co-op until Wednesday, which was market day, and my dad couldn't leave for his country rounds with the grocery orders until they had been made up during the day by the people in the despatch department. That meant he was starting out to villages like Ellisfield at about four o'clock in the afternoon - with a horse-drawn open cart that in the winter time had candle or oil lamps at the front. If it was wet, or frosty, he would use steel "shoes" which hung on chains from the front of the cart, so that he could run the cart on to them, to hold it back as it went down steep slopes. He wouldn't get back to Essex Road till about eleven o'clock at night, sometimes with £100 in his pouch that he had collected for the goods he'd delivered. Then he had to hand in the money and put the horse to bed before he could go home. This was the sort of work pattern that was common in those days. Dad was there for a couple of years.

At the General meeting held on October 16th, 1922 it was reported that a comparison had been made between the costs of delivery by motors and horse-drawn vehicles. "We have three motors, one for deliveries in the Hartley Wintney district and two for deliveries in the country districts from the central Stores." The Chairman stated that the real advantage was that "we were able to deliver farther afield than we should be able to with horses."

Children's Festivals

In 1923 the 22nd annual children's festival was held in the War Memorial Park. Children from outlying districts were brought in by train or motors. The most original fancy dress entrants were Lilian Scutter (bride cake), Joan Barrett (woman's outlook) and Freddy Roomes as "Fred White—he was dressed as a baker advertising Lilywhite flour. This year a feature of the procession to the Park was a parade of the Society's vehicles, decorated for the occasion. There was dancing in the evening "to the strains of the North Hants Ironworks Band" and a concert by the Black and White Minstrel Troupe.

"Gate-crashing"
Lisette Bull

> We didn't belong to the Co-op but we'd heard from the other kids what a lovely time it was and by foul means or somehow or other we got an invite . We thought it was absolutely marvellous sitting on the green and having these lovely sandwiches and cake, it was a real feast to us. We really enjoyed it, it was little things like that that we really did enjoy.

Christmas cakes
Phyl Millar

> When I was a child, I used to go with my Mum into the shop and at Christmas time you could go into the bake-house there and watch them ice the cakes.

Opening hours

In 1924 the Society was asked to consider opening the Stores during the dinner hour but decided against - however, they agreed to open the Grocery, Butchery and Confectionery at 8 am "which would enable parents to send their children for any goods required before going to school."

Goldings

In 1920 the Society made a donation of £50 towards the acquisition of Goldings Park as a War Memorial. This was more controversial than one might expect. A public inquiry was held the following year at the Town Hall concerning the application by the Town Council for sanction to borrow £5,000 for the purchase and adaptation of Goldings.

It appears from the report in the *Hants & Berks Gazette* that there was a "frank exchange of views" during which the Inspector admonished several speakers for rudeness or irrelevance. Mr Tyler spoke for the motion, on behalf of the Basingstoke Co-operative Society. Mr Lewis challenged this, saying he had a petition against the motion signed by members of the Society, but Mr Tyler replied that he had the unanimous support of the Committee, and this was corroborated by the Society's Secretary, Mr H T Andrews. He added that the Basingstoke Co-operative Society "had a considerable standing in the town, doing a trade of £125,000 per annum and having a membership of 2,600. They also had a considerable liability as regards rates."

Goldings Park in 1920

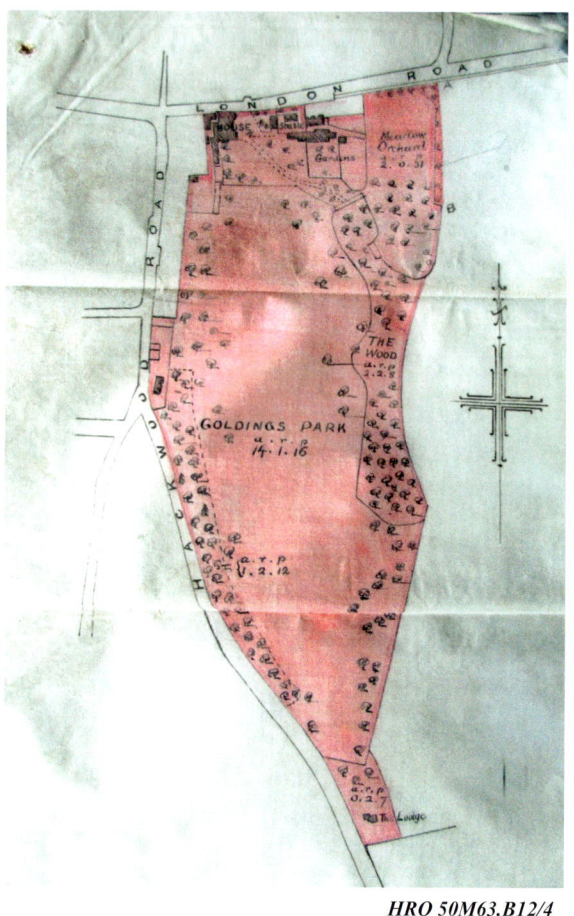

HRO 50M63.B12/4

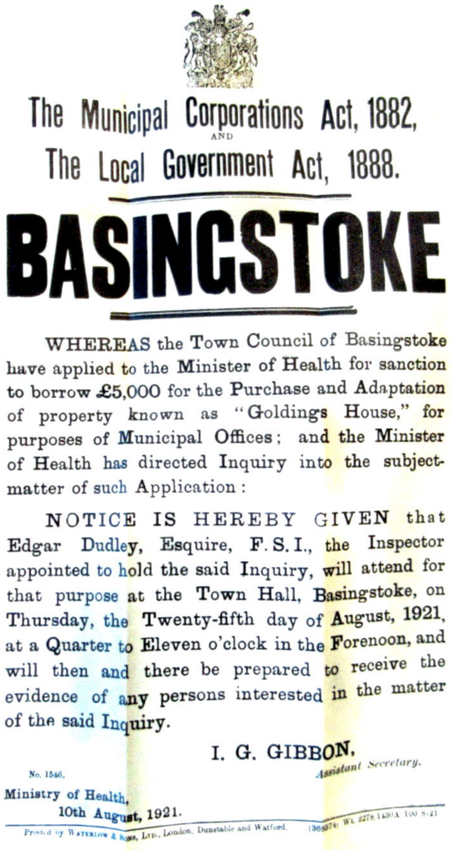

The Council did eventually get the loan and buy Goldings. The house was used for many years as Council offices and is now the Register Office, while the grounds became the War Memorial Park.

HRO50M63/B12/4

Donations

Donations were given to the Alton Cripples Home (£3.3.0) and £2.2.0 each to the Southern Convalescent Home, Basingstoke Hospital, the Hampshire County Hospital and the Royal Berks Hospital.

> In December 1929 the Society made a donation of £5 towards the cost of improvements to the X-ray equipment at the Basingstoke Hospital.

The first X-ray machine in the town had been built by Mr Thumwood and he used it in the Cottage Hospital in Hackwood Road till the outbreak of the First World War, when he went on to a London hospital and someone else took over.

Overseas links

In 1927 the Stores Concert Party gave an entertainment at The Pavilion (the name then given to the Drill Hall in Sarum Hill when it was used as a dance hall),; it was reported to be "completely packed". This was followed by reports of the year's successes, with a membership of over 3,200. Mr Tollerton, the President of the Basingstoke Society, referred to a recent Imperial Conference in London "when many of the Colonial Premiers came over to this country with a view to getting trade relationship on a better footing and endeavouring to get us to take what supplies we could from our Colonies while they in return would take what they could from us." But he boasted that the Co-operative Movement had anticipated that, with depots in Canada, Australia, New Zealand, India and Africa. He went on to say that the development of co-operation in Europe was remarkable. "By trading with one another co-operatively they hoped to understand one another better and so bring about in the future the great ideal of the Co-operative Commonwealth". What would he have thought of the European Common Market and the Euro?

Trade Unions and politics

As early as 1913 the Co-operative Congress, at their meeting at Aberdeen, had "voted approving of concerted action with trade union and other bodies to raise the status of labour, refused to sanction union with the political Labour Party, and instructed the Central Board of the Co-operative Union strictly to maintain the neutrality of the Co-operative Movement."

It was not always clear that the official line was still against overt links with any political party. In 1927 the CWS placed an advertisement in the *Hants & Berks Gazette*.

CO-OPERATIVE WHOLESALE SOCIETY, Limited,
1, Balloon Street, Manchester.

POLITICAL ACTION
IN THE
CO-OPERATIVE MOVEMENT.

To the Society-Members, and to Depositors and others.

Following the decision of the Co-operative Congress, recently held at Cheltenham, approving a proposed agreement with the Labour Party regarding political action, we have received numerous enquiries concerning the position of the C.W.S.

There is apparently considerable misapprehension regarding the situation generally, and particularly as it concerns the C.W.S., consequently we think it desirable to explain our position.

The C.W.S. is not in any way identified with the Labour Party and will not be affected by the Cheltenham resolution.

The C.W.S. does not subscribe to the funds of the Labour Party.

No funds which the C.W.S. holds on behalf of Societies or others can be touched by any outside Party or Movement. In fact, no part of the funds of the C.W.S., or of retail Societies, however small, can be placed at the disposal of any organisation—political or otherwise—without the consent of a Meeting of Members constitutionally assembled.

The C.W.S. is a federation of retail Co-operative Societies, for whom it buys and manufactures.

ITS FUNDS are the property of its Society Members, and are subscribed and used for trading and allied purposes.

Decisions with regard to the local policy of Distributive Societies are quite apart from the C.W.S., whose business is that of PRODUCTION, DISTRIBUTION, BANKING and INSURANCE, for the mutual welfare of the consumers TO WHOM IT BELONGS AND WHOSE INTERESTS IT EXISTS TO SERVE.

THE COMMITTEE

In 1921 Basingstoke had a working population of around 5,800, mainly in engineering, metal-working and transport, so there would be growing interest in trade unions.

In 1924 it was proposed that all Co-op staff should be members of a trade union but it was decided to leave the staff free to decide for themselves whether or not to join.

In 1928 it was proposed that a Co-operative Candidate could be run for the local Town Council. However, the Branch Committee decided to recommended that no action be taken officially.

The Women's Co-operative Guild

Minutes of Committee & Guild meetings for 1920-1927 are held at Hampshire Record Office and give a good insight into the early days. *(112M98/2/1/1/1)*

Whist Drives and children's teas were regular events. In 1920 the total taken at the door for the Whist Drive was £10 3s 3 ½d and expenses were £4 1s 4 ½d, leaving a balance of £5 18s 11d. In 1923 tickets for a whist drive and dance at Church Cottage could be obtained from the Guild Committee for 1s 6d, including refreshments. In November 1924 details were given of catering for the Whist Drive. The Committee went to Church Cottage in the afternoon to cut the sandwiches. Mrs Thelenberg gave the meat for sandwiches, Mrs Taylor gave the butter, Mrs Goodyear gave bread and Mrs Greenway gave ½ gallon of milk. Then for the children's tea in January the following year they had: 6 white loaves & 2 brown loaves, 2 ½ lb butter, 4 lb sugar, ¾ lb tea, 1 gallon milk, 100 small cakes, some seed cake, 3 cherry slab cakes, 3 pink rolls, 7 oranges & 40 apples. Mrs Godwin & Mrs Greenway promised jellies. In 1926 they decided to have a Social at St John's School.

In 1926 the Guild wrote to Mr Waklyn, the Town Clerk, about the bell on the dust cart, but there were more important matters to come up over the years. One chairman did not believe in Politics in the Guild room, it was a mistake to discuss them, but presumably no-one agreed as they continued to consider such questions as a petition about Venereal Disease, Divorce Law Reform, equal franchise for men and women and sending a resolution to the Minister of Education condemning the new education cut.

Papers were read on abolishing capital punishment and on affiliating to the Co-operative Party. In 1929 they considered Nursery Schools and Birth Control and in 1930 the Women's Peace Crusade. The minuted response to a questionnaire on "The Reform of Domestic Work" was, "We feel it does not affect us as most people have conveniences in their own homes."

Members kept a keen eye on matters in the Co-operative Society's shops. In 1922 the Secretary was instructed to write to Mr Tyler about the bad service in the Drapery and Hardware departments and in 1925 he wrote to accept the Guild's suggestion that small quantities of tea and cocoa should be made available for those who could not afford ¼ lb packets, but that a coffee grinding machine would not be provided until there was evidence of demand. He was also asked to come and explain the new Mutuality Scheme.

In 1935 he had to come up again to explain why Management were taking away the room where the Guild met. He said that there was great need of new premises, especially a new bakery, and that the old bakery would be used to store goods and for other purposes. People would not like the store to stand still, the alterations were needed, and the Society was in a good financial position so now was the time to carry them out.

The Guild then tried meeting at The British Workman in Potter's Lane, but they found it too cold. Then enquiries were made about the Mechanics Institute in New Street. Church Cottage was the most favoured option.

The Guild took practical action too. Stamps to the value of 4s 6d were sold for the *Daily Herald's* Maintenance Fund to help miners' children and in 1923 the Chairman suggested sending anything, however small, to go to the Robert Owen's Home for Russian Children who had been orphaned by the famine. The following year they sent a donation towards the demonstrations to be held by the National Council for Prevention of War. The members gave 2d each, which amounted to 3s 2d and Mrs Munday gave the 1d needed to make up the Postage. In 1926 the Guild were informed of a Peacemakers Pilgrimage to begin in May.

In 1925 the Rainbow flag, symbolising the union of peoples, was adopted as an official symbol of the international Co-operative Movement. Later the Co-operative Women's Guild adopted the song "The Rainbow flag"

Unite, and raise the Rainbow flag,
And when it is unfurled
Plant it upon the highest height
And challenge all the world.

The state of the town

To put all this in context, by the end of the 1920s Basingstoke had seen considerable changes. Mr G G Clark, speaking to the Rotary Club in 1930, said, "The whole of this central part of the town, the old north-south road and the great east-west road, has exchanged dwelling houses for shops and business premises. The shopkeeper who used to live above his shop has almost disappeared. He now lives in the suburbs. These are typical of all town suburbs built in the later 19th century and are only saved from disaster by the openness of their planning and the growth of trees which begin to hide them. Without exception they are architecturally uninteresting." He found that the Thornycrofts works had many admirable features. "In the first place, it is a clean industry. " He also approved of a new industry in the town, "the intensive cultivation of tomatoes and cucumbers under glass". He said, "as the buildings are low and smoke and dirt negligible, they should prove an excellent industry from the health point of view." Mr Clark stated firmly, "Basingstoke's future is undoubtedly bound up with the extension of industry . . . Basingstoke is cut out for factories which get their raw material by train or road and despatch it when finished along the same transport routes."

In the villages

In 1929 the Basingstoke Co-operative Society took over the small village Society of Aldermaston, which had 135 members and two staff.

In Hartley Wintney premises known as the Laundry were purchased in Front Street.

In Overton property was purchased in Winchester Street for a new branch.

THE THIRTIES

> ... Population 13,865 (1931) ... Depression ... Eli Lilly & Kelvin Hughes (1938/9) ...

Children's Festivals

The *Hants & Berks Gazette* reported that in 1930 the Co-operative Society's Children's Festival cost approximately £200, "and there can be no doubt but that the money was carefully and wisely expended". The fancy dress competition took place at Essex Road and then the procession, headed by the Basingstoke North Hants Band, went via Church Street, Cross Street, New Street and Victoria Street to Castle Field.

> Immediately upon arrival the most important event of the day took place—the tea. Altogether 2,600 children sat down to tea, their wants being attended to by about 80 helpers. Half the number of children came from country districts, their conveyance to and from the festival by train or bus being arranged and paid for by the Society. The management of this important item alone proves the great organising powers and systematic working of those in charge.
>
> After the tea there was racing for both boys and girls, about £12 being distributed in prizes, while for the children not competing there was an entertainer (Professor Woodley, of Southampton) giving ventriloquial sketches, and general light entertainment. At 6.30, for the older people as well as the younger, there was a concert party from London who called themselves the Crin-Cravats.
>
> During the tea and the evening and later for dancing the band played delightfully, and in addition there were other entertainments, including swing-boats and several side-shows. A large tent was erected, from which teas were dispensed to the adults and there was also another tent where mineral waters and ices could be obtained.

HBG 12.7.1930

Festivals in 1932, 1934 and 1935 followed much the same pattern, with a procession to Castle Field. The *Hants & Berks Gazette* reported in 1934 that there were about 2,500 children, including some from the Old Basing Children's Home, the Vyne Road Boys' Home and women from the Basing Road Institution (the Workhouse). This time the concert party was the Straw Hatters (from Luton) and side shows included the mat slide, the magnetic fish pond, the Ghost House and swings. There were also competitions of boot cleaning (for boys) and spoon cleaning (for girls).

In 1935 "A very great number of people thronged the streets to watch the children marching proudly by." The "A La Carte Concert Party" entertained the older people. In 1938 the Sarum Hill Methodist Band played selections during the afternoon and evening and dance music was provided by Brian Thornton's Silver Prize Accordion Band.

A hunt through the Co-op archives produced this photo of a fancy-dress competition, probably in the 1930s. Unfortunately we don't know where it was but by all accounts the children of Basingstoke had more fun than the children in the photograph. The Co-op must have supplied the advertisements used for fancy dress in the photo, but it seems that Basingstoke parents were more inventive.

I got tea.
Joy Seal

In the 1930s you used to go to the Co-op offices in Essex Road, give your mother's dividend number in at the office - or your grandmother's or anyone you could get - and they gave you an envelope. Girls one pile, boys another, and in it there were about three rolls of crepe paper and a load of labels advertising Co-op goods. You tore it open to wonder what you'd got. Girls usually got jam, tea, marmalade, something like that. I guess the boys had boys' things. Our mums used to make us a fancy dress applicable to whatever we were supposed to be advertising, like strawberry or raspberry jam, where you would have red crepe paper and white.

But I remember very distinctly when I was about seven I got tea. This was brown paper, black paper and white paper and my mother made a little black skirt, a white apron and a little Lyons Corner House hat and I had my dolly tea set on a tray round my neck and all round the thing was hung all kinds of Co-op tea and I got first prize. I don't know who judged it but I know I got first prize. I think it was about something like one and sixpence, which was big money.

And then we used to march all round the yard. My brother recently said to me, 'How did you manage not to tip your tea service over while you were marching?' I don't know. My Mother put tape round the tray and I held the handles. I don't know if it was a proper tray or what. It was a little dolly tea service and she might have stuck it on the tray.

That yard is still there. I think it is industrial units now. We used to march along Essex Road, up Sarum Hill. There wasn't much traffic around those days, but in front of us was a brass band and I am almost certain it was the Brass Band, from the Methodist Church. They had dark red uniforms with gold on them and they marched in front of us and we marched up there, up Victoria Street, up past Fairfields School, turned right by an old First World War tank and we used to go in to what I think is now the playing fields of Fairfields School.

And there we used to have races. It always seemed it was lovely weather - probably wasn't but it was in my memory. Then we would sit at long trestle tables and ladies used to come along with big washing baskets full of lovely crusty bread with butter on it and jam and sponge cake. Mugs of tea or lemonade. This was all free because Mummy used to belong to the Co-op.

HRO 58M74/BP1789

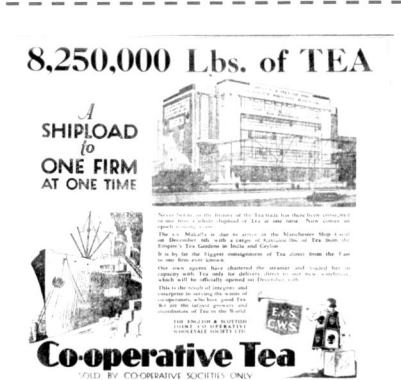

... a milk bottle ...
Pat Wright

Every year there would be a Co-op Party in Budd's Meadow, which is behind where Devonshire Place is now, and we all used to go there and we would have fancy dress sometimes and I can remember all the food, sandwiches and big slab cakes cut up in slices. They would all be brought out in sort of laundry baskets with big white cloths covering them up and then we would have to sit down and wait our turn to be served with the orange juice or whatever and the cake and sandwiches and things.

We used to play games and sometimes we would have fancy dress. You could borrow some from the shop but my aunties were tailoresses. They'd worked in John Mares and so they usually made me one, and one year when I must have been just over five, I can remember Aunty Bet and my Mum dressing me up as a milk bottle and because my sister was very young Mum didn't have time to take me and so they dressed me up as this milk bottle and sent me off to the party, and after Mum had seen me off she turned to Aunt Bet and she said, 'Oh, I hope she doesn't fall over because she'll never get up again!" My arms were down inside the shape of the bottle and I had the white top on the cap on the top and Co-op Milk all across the bottle. That was quite good fun.

55

Essex Road butchery department

A planning application by Messrs Mussellwhite & Son (Eastrop Works) was passed on 24th November 1931 for a new shop front for the butchery department in Essex Road. This was to have brown glazed brickwork to match existing work, teak window frame with ¼" plate glass and lead glazing. Ventilation was by 5" vents at the head of the windows. In the windows the existing
marble shelves were to be re-used, and the marble threshold would include black and

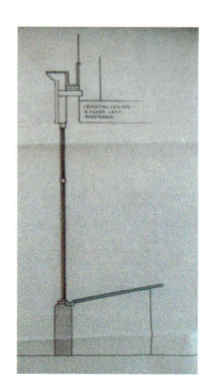

HRO 58M74/BP1789

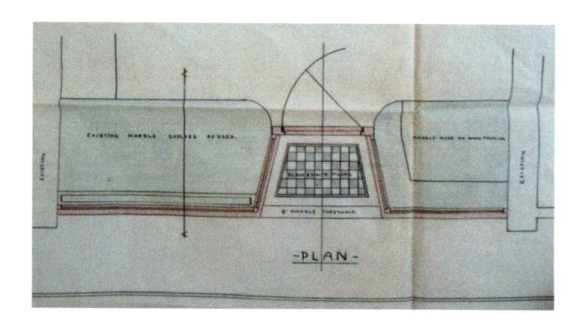

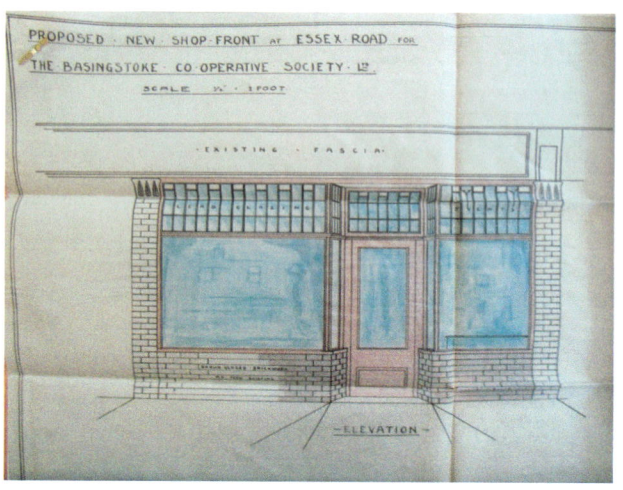

Delivering to the villages …
Joan Mussellwhite

My father was Walter James Sivier and he worked at the Co-op butchers' department in the 1930s, up until the start of the War. His job was to drive a mobile butchers' van around the countryside, visiting the villages to deliver meat. And sometimes I went with him. I have only a vague recollection of it because I was quite young when I did this, but I used to enjoy going round the countryside.

The photograph is of his butchers' van decorated for a Carnival in the 1930s. The Carnivals were held to raise money for a new hospital in Basingstoke. They used to be very exciting, because all the firms decorated floats and it was great fun.

Essex Road Dairy and Warehouse

No sub-editor in those days?
Richard Garfield

> As a *Gazette* journalist, I know I would never be allowed to give such a lengthy and detailed account as this. Words would be strictly counted and the sub-editor's delete button would cut out all the technical information that shows readers how much things have changed since 1933.

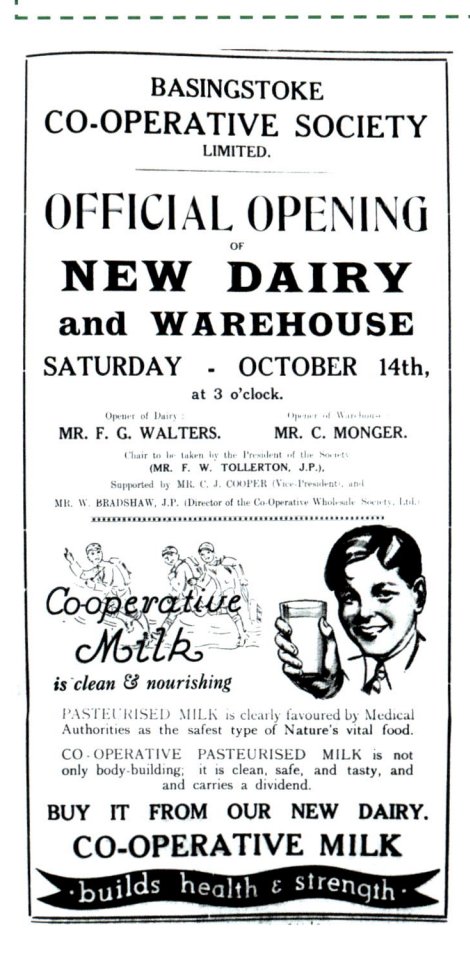

BASINGSTOKE CO-OPERATIVE SOCIETY LIMITED.

OFFICIAL OPENING
OF
NEW DAIRY and **WAREHOUSE**
SATURDAY - OCTOBER 14th,
at 3 o'clock.

Opener of Dairy — Opener of Warehouse
MR. F. G. WALTERS.   MR. C. MONGER.
Chair to be taken by the President of the Society
(MR. F. W. TOLLERTON, J.P.),
Supported by MR. C. J. COOPER (Vice-President) and
MR. W. BRADSHAW, J.P. (Director of the Co-Operative Wholesale Society, Ltd.)

Cooperative Milk is *clean & nourishing*

PASTEURISED MILK is clearly favoured by Medical Authorities as the safest type of Nature's vital food.
CO-OPERATIVE PASTEURISED MILK is not only body-building; it is clean, safe, and tasty, and and carries a dividend.
BUY IT FROM OUR NEW DAIRY.
CO-OPERATIVE MILK
·builds health & strength·

The new buildings were erected by Messrs. Mussellwhite and son, builders and contractors, Basingstoke, to the design of Mr. J. Dolding, manager of the same firm. The warehouse, a red brick building of three stories, is commodious, well lighted, and of a pleasing external appearance. A large electric lift is installed to facilitate the work of moving the stores.

It was the dairy which commanded the greatest admiration. Here the internal walls and some of the floors are finished with tiles impervious to lactic acid, giving a very bright and clean appearance, as well as facilitating cleaning. The floors of the milk receiving room, the platforms, and the cold room, owing to the exceptional wear and tear to which they are subject, are laid in cement, in which cast-iron gratings are embedded.

By the system adopted, which is called the "retarded" or "holding" method, the milk is thoroughly cleaned and then treated to destroy harmful germs, after which it is cooled to preserve its keeping qualities. Milk so treated has no trace of that "cooked" flavour which was noticeable some years ago when it was pasteurised by what is known as the "flash" method.

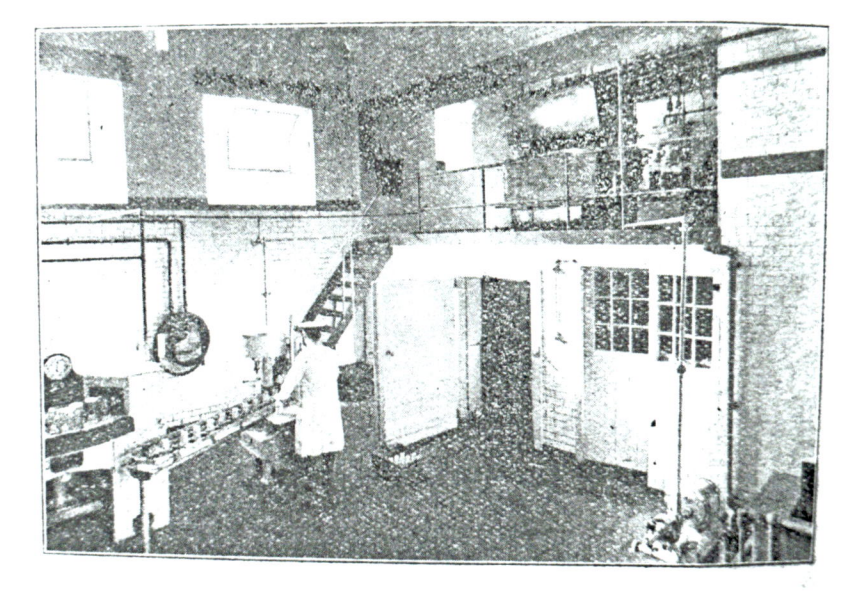

HBG 2010.1933   INTERIOR OF THE NEW CO-OPERATIVE STORES **DAIRY.**

The reporter was greatly impressed by "the most up-to-date pasteurising plant, known as the Unified machine" as well as the modern bottling plant installed by the Graham Knock Manufacturing Co. of Stamford Hill. This could deal with 125 gallons of milk an hour. He went on to describe the process in considerable detail, pointing out that "all surfaces of the machine coming into contact with the milk are made of stainless steel, which can be cleaned without effort, and do not affect the milk in any way, either by corrosion or chemical change. The machine, which heats the milk up to 145 deg. F. and holds it at that temperature for thirty minutes, is fully automatic." The milk then passed through a clarifier and was cooled down to 40 deg. F.

Then he described the bottling plant.

> This machine, which has been officially stamped by a Weights and Measures Inspector, automatically measures the milk, fills the bottles—half-pints, pints or quarts—as required, and caps them with hygienic discs at the rate of 2,100 bottles per hour. The bottles are automatically conveyed to the bottle-filling machine from the bottle-washing machine, the efficiency of which is unrivalled. There are four series of travelling jets inside the machine, the first spraying the inside of the bottles with a warm water rinse, the second with a hot caustic solution, the third with warm water and steam, and the fourth with fresh, cold water from the main. There are also fixed jets for spraying the outside of the bottles. The bottles, immediately they are filled, are placed in boxes and conveyed into the cold room—a large, insulated chamber under the pasteurising floor. From there they are taken out as required to the vehicles for delivery to customers.

As well as the dairy, there was a steam boiler to generate the steam, and a Permutit water softening plant: "All machinery, milk receptacles, walls and floors are washed daily, a number of steam and hot water jets being fixed inside and outside the dairy for this purpose".

Needless, to say, this was the occasion for plenty of speeches, after which a meat tea was enjoyed at the Town Hall by about 80 people, including the delegates from other branches "and afterwards cigars and cigarettes were thoughtfully handed round".

I remember the milkman.
Paul Bosley

> Harry used to work down Essex Road at the old dairy and he used to deliver his milk with the horse. He told me that he wouldn't have to tell the horse to stop, because the horse would know exactly where to start or stop every day on the same round.

Cooperative Milk
is clean & nourishing

Milk is the only complete food in the world. It possesses all the vitamins necessary for building and maintaining healthy bodies. There are, however, dangers with ordinary milk, which may become contaminated through careless handling.

The Pasteurisation of Milk is the only safeguard against infection from tuberculosis, scarlet fever, typhoid, and other diseases, all of which can be disseminated through raw untreated milk.

We, with our modern efficiently-equipped dairy, our vigilant supervision, and our scientific pasteurising plant, are able to guarantee a regular supply of Healthy, Safe and Wholesome Pasteurised Milk, and a useful dividend at the quarter-end.

DRINK CO-OPERATIVE PASTEURISED MILK
FROM THE
BASINGSTOKE CO-OPERATIVE SOCIETY LIMITED

Furniture

Although the 1930s were years of depression, there was an exhibition of CWS furniture in Basingstoke in 1934 which showed modern comforts for the home. The advertisement showed an upholstered armchair, with plump cushions, a reading light well positioned behind it and books within easy reach.

The Central Hall may have been the area which was later to be intended for a furniture department in the plans for 17 New Street.

The following year Queen's Parade was built at the corner of New Street and Flaxfield Road., the corner having "a stucco face with decorated treatment" with paintwork in turquoise blue. Flats contained "up-to-date labour-saving devices", with a dust-hopper to carry dust to a container on the ground floor. One shop was let to Mr Clement Carveth, house furnisher, who provided letting particulars for the shops and flats.

EXHIBITION of C.W.S. FURNITURE
in the Central Hall,
New St., Basingstoke,
from
May 15th to 19th.

All the latest styles and designs in up-to-date home furnishings, made under ideal conditions in your own factories. Don't miss seeing these special displays!

BASINGSTOKE CO-OPERATIVE SOCIETY, LTD.

Coal

He knew about coal.
Glynis Peacock (née James)

I grew up in Essex Road, opposite the main Co-op as it was then. Our house, number 28, was right opposite the men's outfitters.

We came to Basingstoke because of the Co-op. I was born in 1929 in a small village called Oakdale, right in the middle of the South Wales coal fields. My father (William Theophilus James, usually called Theo) was a miner at the local colliery. The men were all laid off in the twenties and there was no work to be had in the area. My uncle, Wilf Dear, had moved to Basingstoke and he found my father a job and a house to rent so, two years old, I came to Basingstoke to live. That was 1931.

The job found for my father was as Manager of the Co-op's coal delivery yard at the back of the stores. He was given the job because he knew his coal, the different grades. He knew what was of good quality. I think that the Co-op had been sold some poor quality coal in the past so they thought it was worth employing an ex-miner who knew his coal. He soon was the main purchaser for other Co-op societies in the area as well as Basingstoke. He would travel down to the Southampton docks and to the large coal yards at railway junctions. I think he even visited collieries, sourcing the coal.

My father's lifetime friend was Nye Bevan. My father used to go to tea at the 'House'.

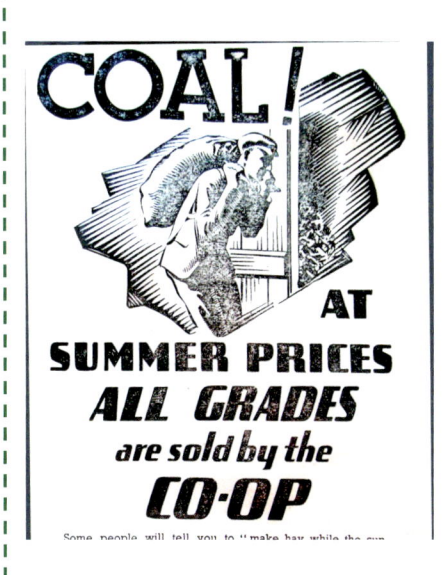

COAL!
AT
SUMMER PRICES
ALL GRADES
are sold by the
CO-OP

A failed attempt

Some time before 1935 the Co-op attempted to set up a store on the Worting Road, described as being "approximately half way between Basingstoke Town Hall and Worting". However, the Council refused planning permission.

This was mentioned by Agostino Dellafera of Flaxfield Road when he appealed against the Council's refusal of his own application to build shops on that site (on the north edge of the pre-WW2 stage of the South Ham estate). He said that there were at present no shopping facilities in the vicinity and this was purely a working-class neighbourhood, "95 % of the residents being of the working class and therefore without the benefit of a telephone for the ordering of goods." He claimed that there were approximately 200 houses in the area, let conditionally to those with the largest families.

However, the Town Planning Officer pointed out that Dellafera's proposed shops would be on the outskirts of the area to be served. The report in the *Hants & Berks Gazette* (January 4 1935) ends with the Inspector about to view the site and report to the Ministry of Health. A shopkeeper, Conellan, is listed near South Ham Road in the 1941 Kelly's Directory, but it was not until the early 1950s that shops were built in South Ham itself and the Co-op store was opened in King's Road.

New shops in New Street

In 1935 two new shops were opened at the corner of New Street and Winchester Street: butchery and confectionery. The Manager, of the Butchery shop, Mr Cyril Wood, later became Mayor of Basingstoke.

The following year Mussellwhite & Sons submitted tenders for work at the slaughter house.

> *for tiling the walls as authorised*   £37. 14. 0.
>
> *for cement washing the walls*   £ 6. 17. 6.

An alternative tender was submitted for painting the walls (£5 16 3) but this must have been too expensive and it was decided just to have them limewashed.

Improved working conditions

A mess room was set up beside the dairy in 1933,

In 1936 a room was made available for the trade union where they could collect contributions when staff received their wages.

In the same year an Employees Social Club was formed. It later included an Employees Cricket Club and an Employees Debating Society.

Adverts

Cheap Food for the People.

Danish Back Bacon	10d,
English refined Lard	7d
English Cheddar cheese	1s 3d
Margarine Red Seal	8d
Butter	1s 1d

Most adverts were for soap! There was President soap, Carbolic soap, and Naptha soap.

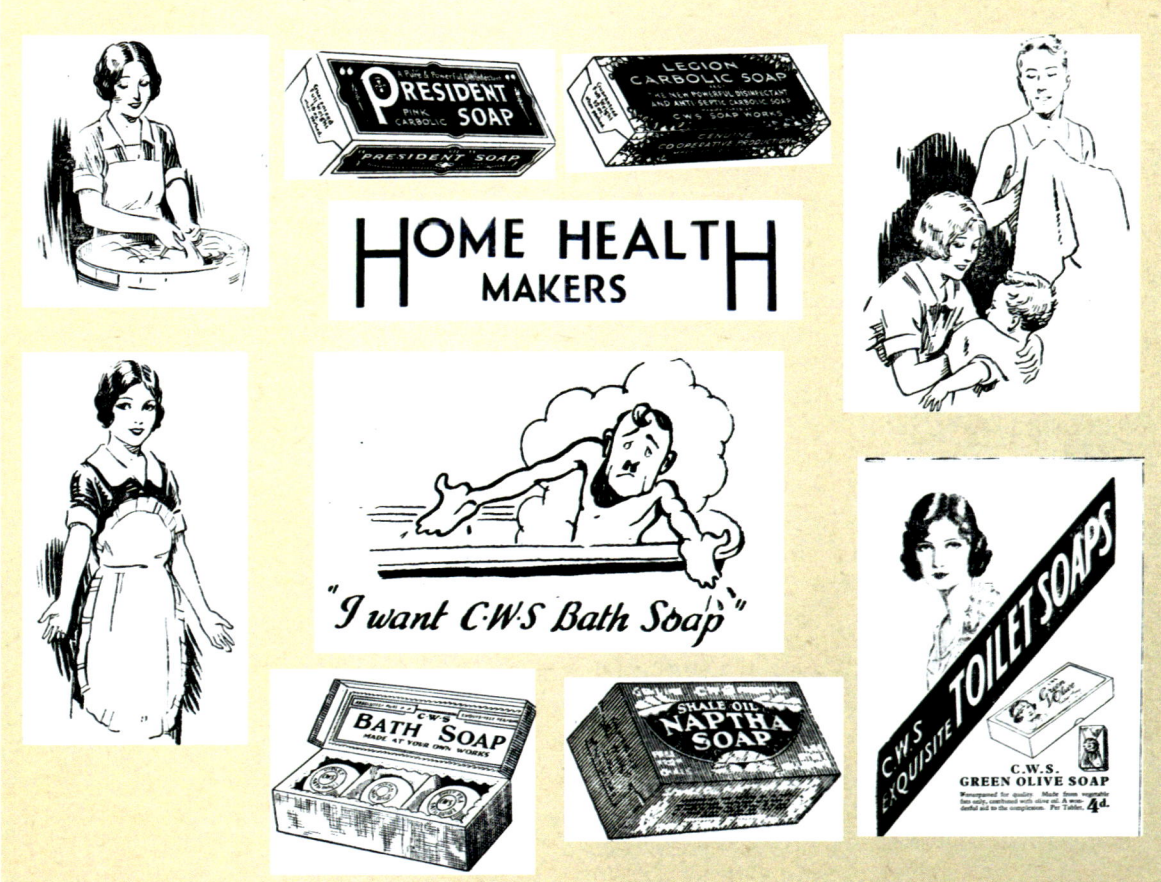

HOME HEALTH MAKERS

"I want C.W.S Bath Soap"

Provisions

Word of mouth ...
Ken Toop

I went to work for the Co-op in 1938. There would be a little card in the window, "Errand boy wanted" or "Shop assistant required". It wasn't difficult to find a job, by word of mouth, even. Somebody would be leaving, perhaps, and you'd hear of it and you'd come.

I worked with Mr Stannard. The other men there were older, there was Mr Baughurst, Mr Dannimore, Mr Pannett, Mr Levy. A young woman, I believe her name was Miss Webb, used to look after all the order books which people used to bring in or shove through the letter box. This was the way it was done. You wrote out your order in a book, shoved it through the letter box, then it was made up for you and delivered by the errand boy, or if it was out in the country by the van, I used to have to go in there by eight o'clock in the morning. They started cashing up before shutting about six o'clock at night.

It was quite a modern shop really. It was tiled all round - but of course before the War, like all grocers' shops, it wasn't self-service. You went in and asked for what you wanted and the counter-hand made it up in front of you and when he'd weighed it all and priced it all he put it in a bag for you, tied it up with sugar string, you went on your way or you had it delivered later on in the day.

All the butter was in half hundredweight blocks and it had to be knocked out on a marble slab with two butter pats and then knocked into shape, and weighed up on a piece of greaseproof paper to the correct weight on the scales manually every time anybody wanted any butter.

The butter pats had indentations on them, sometimes a cow or a sun or some pleasing design and this was then printed on the butter. And then the butter pats would be put back in a bucket of cold water until the next time. This was going on all the time, knocking up butter. If there was a slack period the provision hands would be doing this. And then the cheeses came in two fifty-six pound cheeses in one box, which was one hundredweight, plus the box weight. And these had to be skinned, because a proper cheese is in skin, in muslin, you see, and it's all got to be skinned before it's cut and scraped off, of course.

And then on the dry side, all the currants and the dried fruit came in wooden boxes and on a Monday three or four hands would knock this out and loosen it up on the counter. And then they used to have half a pound, or a pound, whatever you were weighing up, and pack it up in blue paper - it was quite common in the grocery trade, blue paper, about 10 inches square, and you weighed your fruit into the centre of a square piece of paper, and folded it and pressed in the ends and then pressed in the other end. It was a very skilled job, but easily learned and some of the people were very fast at it. Because you had a lot to do. You had the currants, sultanas, prunes, soda, everything was done like this. And then this stuff was all stacked in a fitment ready for selling. Now, of course, with pre-packing it's all done by machines somewhere else.

The girls used to do the bookwork, checking the orders and making up the totals and all that.

You weren't designated to do one thing and that only. I used to go between the New Street Co-op and the despatch department at the bottom in Essex Road, where the Co-op had their dairy for their bottling, their bakery, where they did all the bread and cakes and everything else, because they had a vast round. And I was always down there at the warehouse getting stuff which we'd run out of, or getting the tokens.

There was a lot of token trade done then. You had tokens for your bread and milk. When they put their order in people used to order 20 tokens or however many they wanted, and they would pay for them with their grocery order. And then they would just put one out for the milkman or whatever they wanted every morning. This was the way it was done.

And the purchases used to give a dividend (the "divi"), which could be quite a lot of money at the end of the half year if the dividend was a shilling and sixpence in the pound, and a lot of people were picking up £5, £7 a half year - well, this was a lot of money then. A lot of people relied on dividend to buy shoes or whatever they wanted.

There was competition, of course. There was Tempest Leate's in Church Street and at the top of the town there was Home & Colonial, Liptons, International Stores, Wards, and Tyrrell, Smith & Grippers in Wote Street. There were a lot of grocers, but the Co-op, I think, had the biggest organisation in Basingstoke. Their stuff was reasonably priced and you had the divdend, this was the thing. You felt that you were getting part of the profit back.

1938-1939

BASINGSTOKE Co-operative SOCIETY LTD.

There was a great change in 1938 and early 1939. Suddenly there were Co-op adverts in the *Hants & Berks Gazette* every week, and they illustrated a much greater variety of goods. There is a theory that as the country came out of depression the threat of war brought new jobs in armaments, and more work brought more buying power: "unfortunately war is money", in the short term at least. People were concerned not just with food and clothing but with health, cleanliness, safety and leisure activities.

The Co-op placed advertisements in other publications too.

> **Basingstoke Co-operative Society Ltd.**
>
> TELEPHONE: BASINGSTOKE 27
>
> OUR REFERENCE B/J.
>
> YOUR REFERENCE _____
>
> Registered Office:
> Essex Road,
> Basingstoke,
> Hants.
>
> 22nd October, 1938.
>
> Mr. W. A. W. Jarvis,
> 10, Cromwell Road,
> Basingstoke.
>
> Dear Sir,
>
> We enclose herewith cheque value 15/- in payment of our advertisement for the St. Mary's Eastrop Parish Magazine as stated in your letter of the 14th inst., We shall be glad if you will continue our advertisement throughout 1939.
>
> Yours faithfully,
>
> *Receipt Sent 24/10/38.*
>
> G. Haddock
> Secretary.
>
> GH/NH.

The Mayor's car

My mother went as Mayoress.
Glynis Peacock (née James)

> My uncle, Wilf Dear, was Mayor in 1938-1939. As a working man he did not have a car but the Co-op used to lend one of their cars for civic events and then my Father would be chauffeur. It was a family event because my Aunt did not like going to "big do's" so my Mother would go as Mayoress.

The previous Mayor was Mrs Edith Weston, the first female Mayor of Basingstoke. The one before was William Henry Musellwhite, builder, whose firm had done so much work for the Co-op. Mr Dear was followed by William Doswell and Henry Thornton, baker.

WARTIME AGAIN

1939-1945

... Bombs (1940 /41) ...   War work at factories, 2500 employed at Thornycrofts ...

The first announcement that war had been declared with Germany was on the radio on 3rd September 1939. On 8th September the *Hants & Berks Gazette* printed the King's speech to his peoples. On the opposite page was an advertisement for the new CWS DEFIANT radio. It may be that this name simply reflected the Co-op's defiance of other manufacturers by producing their own brand, but it does seem particularly appropriate at this time.

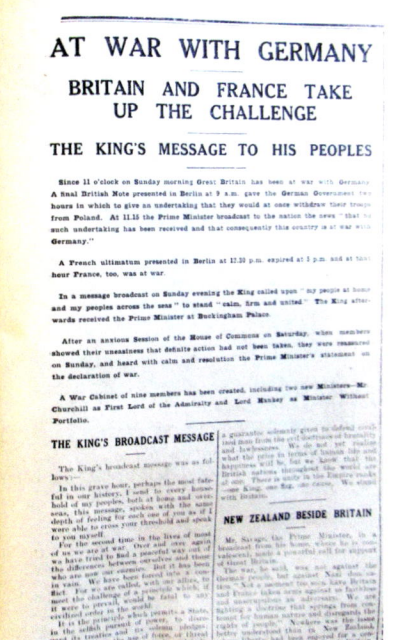

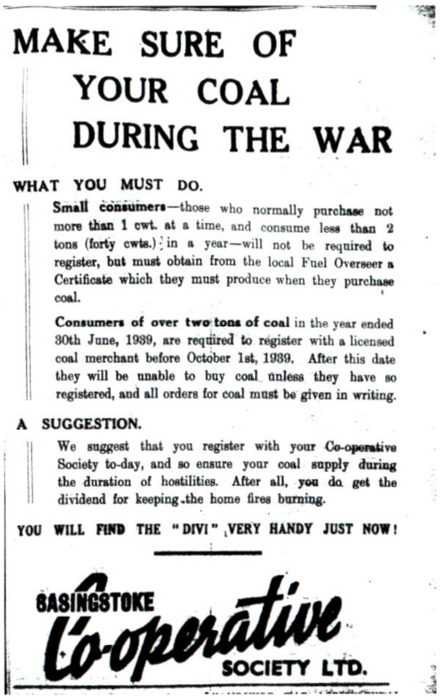

Already that August the Co-op had responded to wartime restrictions on the purchase of coal. As the year progressed they assured customers that they had made plans for difficult times.

Part of Eli Lilly was commandeered for aircraft instrument manufacture by Kelvins, while Wallis & Steevens produced road rollers for airfield construction and Thornycrofts produced bren-gun carriers and aircraft parts in addition to their more traditional lorries.

The first year of the war saw the retirement of the President of the Basingstoke Co-operative Society, Mr F W Tollerton, JP and the Vice-President, Mr C J Cooper. Each had served for over 25 years, and the occasion was marked by a what the *Hants & Berks Gazette* called "a very pleasing ceremony" when the employees presented them with canteens of cutlery. Mr Tollerton said that during his term of office he had helped to steer the society through one world war "and now we were in another, and he hoped that we should still maintain good progress until the victorious end."

Anywhen until midnight ...
Phyl Millar

When I was about 17 I started work in the Despatch Department in Essex Road. There were about seven of us in Despatch. We had all the delivery men that used to do parcels and I used to check the parcels out and they would go in the different piles to be delivered by motor van out to Oakley, Old Basing, Herriard, all the way round. Once a year we used to do stock-taking, and this would mean working there anywhen until midnight. After that I worked in the shop. I used to take the money for the despatch orders and serve as well.

I was there in 1939 when the war broke out. We had gas masks and there was a big sort of cellar at the back where you could go if an air raid was on.

Wills cigarette card

As rationing was imposed, newspapers printed Ministry advice on what to eat and how to prepare it.

Carrot Sandwiches for a change

1. Add two parts of grated raw carrot to one part of finely shredded white heart of cabbage, and bind with chutney or sweet pickle. Pepper and salt to taste.
2. Equal amounts of grated raw carrot, cabbage heart and crisp celery bound with chutney or sweet pickle. Pepper and salt to taste.
3. Bind some grated raw carrot with mustard sauce, flavoured with a dash of vinegar.
4. Cook diced carrot in curry sauce until tepid enough to spread easily with a knife.

All these fillings taste their best with wholemeal bread.

The Hants & Berks Gazette carried Ministry of Food adverts encouraging readers to try out new fish, since zoning schemes had been imposed for fishing. Interestingly, they didn't give the names of the new fish, just describing them as round white fish (cousins of the cod) and flat fish.

FOOD FACTS

Meet the new fish

Strange new fish on the fishmonger's slab — fish you've never met before, but well worth knowing all the same.

You get these new fish because of the zoning scheme: fish is now sold close to where it is landed instead of being sent far journeys to its old markets.

There are two kinds of strangers, *round white fish* (cousins of the cod), and *flat fish*. It it well worth while to look out for them in case they come your way. And don't judge them by their outlandish names or unfamiliar looks—beauty in a fish isn't skin deep!

These newcomers have a fine flavour, are an economical food and are quick and easy to cook. Just follow the instructions given here:

CLEANING FISH

1. Wash fish thoroughly, under running water if possible.
2. Never skin fish before cooking, you lose so much goodness. After cooking remove skin only if very tough.
3. Cut off heads and tails before boiling or frying, but leave on for baking. Use head and bones for stock.

FILLETING FLAT FISH

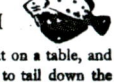

When fish has been cleaned and dried, place flat on a table, and with the point of a *sharp* knife cut from head to tail down the backbone. Then insert knife in this slit and carefully separate the fish from the bone. Remove fillets, trim and cut into pieces convenient for serving. Use bones for stock.

BOILING FISH

Steam whenever possible, but if you must boil, place fish in warm, salted water. Bring to boiling point and then simmer gently. Never boil fast or the fish will come away from its bones before it is properly cooked, and may be tough. Drain fish well before serving and use liquid for sauce.

FRYING FISH

1. Fish must be perfectly dry before frying. Put it in a dry cloth and press gently before frying. Dip in a very little seasoned flour or roll in oatmeal.
2. Use enough fat to prevent fish sticking to bottom of pan.
3. Let fat give off blue smoke before putting in fish.
4. Fry quickly on both sides.

LISTEN TO THE KITCHEN FRONT EVERY MORNING AT 8.15

THE MINISTRY OF FOOD, LONDON, W.1. FOOD FACTS No. 121

The Ministry also reported on the food given to young children in war-time nurseries.

They admitted that "the world position in regard to butter production is becoming somewhat serious" since the present supply position (1944) was only just enough to maintain the ration at 2 oz a week.

A quantity of bitter oranges had arrived from Spain. This was enough for the English jam manufacturers with some left for "some lucky housewives who had a small amount of sugar stored away" to be able to make their own marmalade again.

Travelling demonstrators were giving special cookery talks demonstrating a range of dried egg dishes.

MINISTRY OF FOOD NOTES

CHILD WAITERS

The feeding of young children in war time nurseries is proceeding very satisfactorily. The youngsters have become accustomed to and like the well balanced and nutritive diets which are offered them. Salads, made of vegetables with their rich vitamin C content, are extensively used on the nursery dining tables, among them being lettuce, carrots, cabbage, swedes, new beetroot, parsley, tomatoes, mustard and cress, raw marrow, spring onions, potatoes, beans and peas. Some of the toddlers are taught to help their fellows by taking turns in waiting on each other. The general health of young children in the country is good and is largely due to planning by the Ministries of Food and Health and of local authorities.

Basingstoke Co-operative Society
1941 Kelly's Directory for Basingstoke

Registered offices Essex Rd
Grocers 16 & 17 New Street and 28 & 30 Winchester Street
House furnishers 15 New Street
Coal depot Great Western & Southern Railways goods yards, and Lower Brook Street

EVERY ENDEAVOUR

WILL BE MADE TO ENSURE CO-OPERATIVE SERVICE AND—

—YOU WILL ALWAYS BE ABLE TO RELY ON C·W·S PRODUCTIONS

Your safeguard—the letters C·W·S
Pure and wholesome always

BASINGSTOKE Co-operative SOCIETY LTD.

MINISTRY OF WAR TRANSPORT
MINISTRY OF FOOD · BOARD OF TRADE

Customers and shopkeepers in big patriotic effort

If customers will carry their shopping home they will be doing their country a real service. They will also be helping their shopkeepers who are re-planning their delivery service, so that there will be even more man-power, petrol and rubber to put paid to Hitler and his followers.

You may find this scheme a little tiresome, but it will run far more smoothly and happily for every-one concerned if you will give it your whole-hearted support. And you will help to shorten the war.

IMPORTANT NOTICE TO RETAILERS

Watch out for notice of meetings called by the Sub-district Transport Manager, or the Local Food Executive Officer of your area. You will be asked to attend these meetings in order to assist in the plans for the reorganisation of delivery services, which may involve the pooling of vehicles, deliveries of goods on certain days only, or the restriction of delivery areas.

The war brought shortages of paper and other materials, as well as censorship, and it is noteworthy that a bound volume of the *Hants & Berks Gazette* for the years 1943-1944 was thinner than one for any year in the 1930s. So it is not surprising that the only advertisement placed by the Basingstoke Co-operative Society in those years was for war-time Utility furniture, quite a change from the comfortable chair shown in 1934 (page 59). By now the furnishing department was in Winchester Street.

BASINGSTOKE CO-OPERATIVE SOCIETY, Ltd.

Your enquiries about **UTILITY FURNITURE** will be welcome, and orders will receive prompt attention on production of permit for same.

We shall also be pleased to buy SECOND-HAND FURNITURE. Best prices and prompt cash given.

FULL DIVIDEND on all PURCHASES

All enquiries to —
FURNISHING DEPARTMENT,
WINCHESTER ST., BASINGSTOKE.

The Co-operative Women's Guild

In December 1939 members of the Co-operative Women's Guild discussed a paper sent from Head Office about Armistice Day celebrations (presumably proposing to suspend these on the outbreak of War that year), but their Minute books for the next years make no mention of rationing, shortages, blackout or any other inconveniences. This may have been the effect of censorship.

Later they decided to send a letter to the American Embassy on behalf of members asking for a cease fire and for negotiations and withdrawal of all foreign troops from South East Asia.

By April 1945 it was possible to think of the future.

Like the Co-operative Bank, the Co-operative Insurance Society was a sister organisation of the national Co-operative. In the 1941 Kelly's Directory its offices are above Gribble, Booth & Shepherd, auctioneers, next to Victoria Street. The district manager was Mr A E Watkins.

START BUYING YOUR FUTURE HOUSE NOW.

There are no snags in the C.I.S. Plan. Safe, simple and economical. For details write :—

CO-OPERATIVE INSURANCE SOCIETY·LTD

District Office:
37a, Winchester Street,
BASINGSTOKE.
Assets exceed £51,500,000.

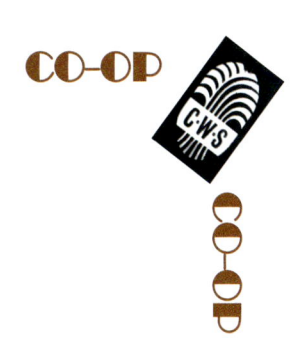

AFTER THE WAR AND THE FIFTIES

... Population 16978 (1951) ... Lansing Bagnalls (1949) ... AWRE (1950) ...

Rationing continued

Rationing was still in place for some years after WW2, and on December 17th 1948, in a letter to the Editor of the *Hants & Berks Gazette*, Mr A Lovick, the Managing Secretary of the Co-operative Society, answered criticism in the national press that the Co-op was being allocated more than its fair share of rationed sugar, rabbits and poultry.

The controversy was related to the distribution of extra supplies available post-war, which were to be divided by the Ministry of Food according to pre-war statistical methods, since they had failed to arrive at a reasonable alternative.

A fair allocation

He said that in fact, regarding sugar and flour for confectionery, the national Co-operative Movement was entitled to more on this basis, since its membership of customers had increased from 8.4m in 1938 to 10m in 1948. The extra allocation of 2.7 thousand tons of sugar and 2.25 thousand tons of confectionery flour (in both cases 23% of the total available) was therefore fair.

Mr Lovick also pointed out that the Co-op had been getting less than 10% of flour for bread, whilst supplying 25% of the total national bread consumption, and the national Co-op registrations for the sugar ration were more than one quarter of the population.

Regarding extra imported rabbits and poultry (the shortfall being due to feed shortages) he felt that the Co-op should receive more than its allocated 4.5% of the total, since it now represented 10% of consumers.

In local terms, trade had increased by £200,000 per annum in the last ten years, with an increased membership of 3,000 and it was still expanding.

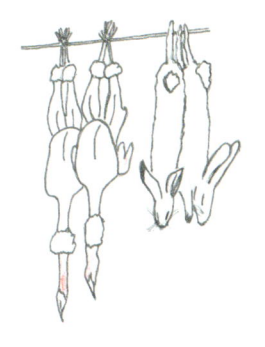

So he maintained that the distribution of extra supplies on the basis of pre-war data was inadequate and unfair, and that commercial interests should secure a good alternative method. Members of the public should not "take notice" of distorted statements.

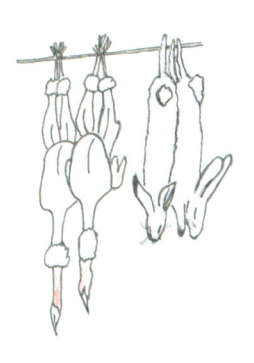

The Mutuality Club

Until I got married in 1953 . . .
Joan Hobbs

I worked on the Mutuality Club, where you paid a deposit and then a shilling a week. It was only up to £15, but £15 was a lot of money in the 1940s. When you paid five shillings you were given £5's worth of vouchers, £1 on a page and you could tear them in half for ten shillings. You could spend them, and you paid a shilling in the pound, like five shillings a week until it was cleared. If you went over, and if you didn't pay it by a set date you lost your deposit. So that was a lot of ledger work.

I used to go and help pay out the "divi". I wasn't the cashier but I used to write on a voucher out of the customer's pass book how much she was going to have, £2, £3, whatever. And then they took it to the cashier and she paid them the money. There were always queues and we used to go to Overton, Hartley Wintney, Kingsclere, and I think it was every six months. But then they took the "divi" part to Portsea Island down Portsmouth way so we didn't do that in Basingstoke, and it gradually fizzled out. Which was a shame.

The office was quite big because you had different departments in there. You had Coal, you had Mutuality, which I was on, and then you had the Check Office, there was the Milk, somebody in charge of all the milkmen. Then you had the bakery men as well, they had somebody in charge of them so it was quite a big place in Essex Road. It's still there, the building, but of course it's been made up to lots and lots of units, there's an upholsterer, there's the television mender, I think there's a car mechanic, and it's all different people there now.

I did love that job and made lots of friends. I still talk to people in the town that I met there.

From milk to fish

I wasn't keen on horses . . .
Gwen Candy

My first job was to count out the milk tokens. At that time the milk and bread were delivered by horse and cart and I used to have to go down to the yard to collect the tokens from the deliverymen, which I didn't like because I wasn't keen on horses.

Soon afterwards I was in charge of balancing the milkmen's books, and a short while later I was moved across the road to the Fish Department to balance up their books. That was a smelly job!

Despatch and Deliveries

...*a lot of people*...
Joan Hobbs

A lot of people worked at the Co-op. There were roundsmen who picked up people's order books and brought them back to the Despatch Department. They did up all the groceries that were wanted, and these would be delivered, and then the roundsmen went back and picked the money up, and picked up the order for the following week. So that would be a week in advance of what you wanted.

They had their own mechanics, and they had bakers. There was a big Bakery Department. There was a Grocery Department, and there was a Shoe Shop, Greengrocery Shop, Ladies' Clothes, Men's Outfitters, and a Butcher's Shop, so you imagine, having a group of people with each department, there must have been quite a lot of people.

£3 a week for eight hour days...
Anne Clarke

It was a very good place to work. I loved it down there. There were never any arguments and no-one ever fell out with each other. They treated me really well and showed me what to do. It was all on first name terms and with none of that "I'm in charge, you will do what I say" attitude.

We used to sing songs all day and sometimes someone would bring in a ball and suddenly, whack, they'd throw it at you, but it was only in fun.

In the despatch department we used to make up customers' orders, which were delivered to their homes. We each had our own section - I had things like tins of peas, cornflakes and Oxo cubes, which I'd put in boxes that went round to us on a roller system.

As a box came to me I would take out an order book and look on the list to see what was needed. Ticking off the list, I would place the goods and the book back in the box and then send it on to the next person. Eventually it went to the checkout where the goods were all added up and packed.

Then it would be sent to the loading bay and the delivery man would open the big doors and take the boxes and load them onto the van and deliver them.

I got paid £3 a week for eight-hour days. But £3 was quite a bit in those days for a young person. When you got older it went up to £5 and then £8.

When you worked there you had to learn everything about the grocery trade. I had to learn all about fruit and veg, how to slice and salt bacon and skin a cheese - they always seemed to get me to skin a cheese.

We also had to go out to every Co-op in the area. I remember going to the Co-op in Overton and also in Oakridge, which used to be a caravan, where Tesco Express is now. It was really nice to go to different places.

Sometimes I would have to help with deliveries. I used to dread it. I remember going out to farms in Old Basing with this bloke early one morning in a Co-op van. It had been snowing all day and we went along some old tracks - there were no housing estates there then. The snow got worse and worse and we got stuck in a snowdrift. The delivery man had to ask a farmer to get a tractor to get us out. I didn't get home until 6 pm - I was frozen stiff. When I look back at it now, it seems funny, but at the time it wasn't much fun.

I left the Co-op after 11 years, aged 26 - my happiest days at work.

I really loved the electric milk float.
Alan Andrews

My father's round in the 1950s started from the depot in Essex Road along Worting Road, and what was then South Ham, which would have just been Sandys Road, Aldworth Crescent and part of Western Way, round to St Patrick's Road, Princes Crescent. That was all that existed; the rest of all around us was farm land. I got to know the round well because I used to go out with him to "help". I really loved the electric milk float, though they were not very big - you could only get about a hundred bottles in it. Most people paid with the tokens, which they would leave out with the empty bottles. That was fine in the summer but not so good in the cold weather, especially because some people would put the tokens in the bottle and it would ice up. We used to take the bottles and swill them out with warm water, trying to dislodge the token.

They'll teach you to drive.
Kath Sanders

In 1945 when I was 28 I became a Co-op driver. I went down to the Labour Exchange to see what was about. The only job there was the Co-op who wanted a driver. I said, "Well, I can't drive." "They'll teach you!" Teach me! Yes - I should think they did teach me! I had a bull-nose Morris 10 cwt to start with. A lovely old van it was too. I liked that old van. But it didn't have a starter. So every time you stopped the van you had to swing the starting-handle.

The driver took me out the first week to teach me the rounds. I did drive a little way, not very much.

And the second week, he was going to teach me to drive. And he came along on the Tuesday morning. He said, "This is my last day. I've got to go out and do some rounds for people who are away sick. So here's the car. Get on with it." And that was my learning!

I had two rounds to do, one one day, one on another day, all the way through the country. From Basingstoke Co-op itself. Odiham Co-op was part of Basingstoke - it was a branch, so I used to come in to Basingstoke Co-op, put my order in, load all my own bread, and about twenty bottles of milk for outlying people, and some meat. I always had a tray of cakes on the van. And I'd go on a long, long way through the houses, it wouldn't pay them now to do it, but we did it.

I enjoyed doing it, I enjoyed the people. I made a wonderful lot of friends there. And, as with most of my jobs, I've been free of other people. I've worked on my own. I've been responsible.

I did have quite a few problems at different times. One time the gear lever had been welded on, but badly, and it came off in an awkward position, by Hook Post Office. I stopped because I couldn't do anything else with it.

I used to have to come into Basingstoke every morning, get the bread, go back out to Odiham. Coming down Wellocks Hill one morning the back wheel came off. I was lucky. It was the near side. And the van went up on the kerb. And we lost the wheel, couldn't find the wheel. It had gone over the hedge! There was a cottage there and I asked them to phone up, tell them I was stranded there and they came out and fetched me.

And one time in 1947 I got a smash. I was on the way from Swanmore. I was going along towards the Alton Road towards the Golden Pot, there was a farm and you went up and sort of looped round, went up and came down another road. We were going to Powntley's Copse. I only went there twice a week, it was a weekend and the van was full of bread so it was fairly heavy and I had just come down onto the main road. I was going slowly and there was a bend, and round this bend at speed came a big Cheviot lorry and he caught me. He was travelling! He couldn't stop. I was almost stopped and the weight of my bread held me. He knocked the front of the van in. I didn't get hurt but just very very scared.

But the funniest thing, of course, it blocked the road up, this van, and about five minutes later along this road came a timber wagon. They put their brakes on and the timber just went over the hedge behind me. It was most pretty to watch!

Anyway, the boys in the van took me into South Warnborough, and I phoned up. I had to wait two hours and these boys waited with me on the road. We had a fire in a bucket, in a tin. And the Co-op brought me out a little 5 cwt van. And I was so scared I wouldn't let the mechanic go. He put my bread into the van he'd brought out and I took him with me all that day.

I nearly got killed in another van they gave me. Coming along from Odiham, going up through South Warnborough, there used to be a big tree in the middle of the road, if you turned the corner. And at the top of this bit of road, it was a Y - a big Y, you couldn't see round, either side, and the house stood there with a privet hedge about 7 foot high hanging over the road. And it was a beautiful May morning, lovely as it is out here, beautiful, and I was at peace with the world, coming up there, I didn't have to stop at those houses that day because I only called twice a week at these houses. And somebody said in my ear, "Nancy bus!" I pulled over and Nancy bus came round that corner at forty miles an hour. Oof! And I'm always sure someone sitting behind me said, "Nancy bus!" Nancy bus was the name of our local bus. It came round the corner about forty miles an hour. I drove very carefully the rest of the day, I believe I did.

A small order ...
Catherine Metcalfe

The Co-op that we used was the Co-op in Essex Road, and we had a delivery from there every week and also an order from the butcher in Essex Road. The butcher at that time was a man called Cyril Woods, who was also a Labour councillor, if I remember rightly. The order was delivered during the week, and I am amazed now what a small order it was. A very small cardboard box with a quarter of tea, a small bag of sugar, etc. With the meat that came from the Co-op, those were mainly the things that we lived on during the week.

We did have a bread order also from the Co-op and his name was Mr Catchpole, and he came several times a week with a very large basket, knocked on the door and there was a large selection of different loaves of bread - never wrapped, of course, just given to you in your hand, but nevertheless a very good selection.

The row of shops ...
Glynis Peacock (née James)

Next to the Mission chapel was the Bakery then the Butcher's, the Grocers and then the Outfitters.

Later the order of shops changed from time to time.

Doing the shopping

A little chit with the number on it ...
Catherine Metcalfe

5992, my mother's Co-op number. I can remember going into the shop and buying things and having to say the number and being given a little chit, usually yellow, with the number written on it.

The life blood ...
Margaret Hayward

I lived in May Street and we shopped at the Essex Road Co-op, which was the life blood for the bottom of the town, with the bank above.

Waving to my aunt ...
Bob Applin

I used to do the shopping for my mother in the 1950s. She'd write out the order in her order book and I'd put that in one of the bags I hung on the handlebars of my bike. I'd ride over the railway bridge, along the Worting Road and along Essex Road to the Co-op shops at the end.

There'd probably be a queue and while I was waiting I would wave to my aunt sitting in the cashier's booth. When it was my turn I gave the order book to the assistant, who got all the goods from the shelves or from a store at the back and ticked them off in the book. I would load the shopping into the bags, hook the bags onto the handlebars and cycle home.

Self-Service

The first self-service shop in Great Britain was at Southsea and there the Portsea Island Mutual Co-operative Society (PIMCO) produced promotional material to explain to the public how this new idea worked.

For many years the layout was standardised for all self-service branches so that customers would be able to find their goods in any PIMCO store.

"Self-Service is Quick Service"

Learning the prices ...
Ken Toop

My wife, Lil, went to work at the Co-op in 1946. The first self-service shop in Basingstoke was the top Co-op when it was in New Street. The very first one. My wife and another woman at the till at the door used to take all the purchases off the people and mentally add up the prices. But the prices weren't marked on the article, they were marked on the fittings. And so they had to know the price of everything in the shop. They had to be conversant with everything from small items to Zeebo grate-powder, or whatever it was, every solid thing.

When they started to go over to this, Lil used to say to me, "I don't think I'll ever be able to learn this." I said, "Yes you will, you'll manage it all." And I used to say things to her like "Six matches" or "99 Tea", or whatever, evening times and that when we were on our own, and she used to fire the price back at me. It's amazing the mind she had for prices. She knew every single item, there was hardly anything she didn't know the price of in that shop. And she got so used to people saying their numbers that she would meet them in the street and completely forget their names but know their numbers, their dividend numbers. Isn't that marvellous!

GOOD MORNING MRS. 1291.

The cash office

How I met my husband ...
Gwen Candy

When I worked at the cash office I had my eye on this young lad in the grocery department. He was a nice-looking lad. I suppose he looked at me and I looked at him. Cash was put in cups or canisters, like big eggs, along with a ticket with the customer's divi number and sent on the wire-and-pulley system to me. I would note this down and send back change. I used to receive little notes from Reg this way. Sometimes the note would be an invitation to the cinema or perhaps to go for something to eat. Sometimes he used to put a cube of sugar in so that I could have sugar in my tea - he was sweet like that.

I left after three years but I had enjoyed working at the Co-op. I got paid 19 shillings a week and used to give my mother 10 shillings, keeping the other nine for myself. That was quite a lot in those days, especially when you think that a loaf of bread cost fourpence ha'penny.

Nellie Lawford gave me valuable advice.
Gerry Traynor

I first met Nellie around 1952 when I joined the Labour Party. She was a well loved local Councillor and later became Mayor. I was a little in awe of her, she was a large lady with a large personality. I soon found that she had a large heart as well. She loved the people of Basingstoke and spent her whole life working for the Community. Each day she was at work in the Finance Office of the Co-op, that was upstairs in their offices in Essex Road. If anyone had a problem they would go to see her there and she would stop what she was doing and see what she could do to help.

She was instrumental in my becoming a Councillor and she gave me some valuable advice which I still remember and attempt to adhere to. She said, "Never give empty promises. If you promise you will do something for a constituent DO IT. If it is not possible, go back and explain why not."

She was a good and skilful Chairman. Her meetings always ran well. Years later I also had the privilege to be a Justice of the Peace with her on the Basingstoke Bench. I always enjoyed working with her. She was always firm but fair. She helped me in many ways during my early years.

Nellie Lawford and the Queen ...
Criss Connor

When the Queen visited Basingstoke, the then Mayor, Cllr Alan Turner, introduced her to several prominent local people. In this photo she has just passed Nellie Lawford, who is standing next to her tall husband, with Councillor Len Smart beyond.

The story is that Nellie had met the Queen on a previous occasion and when she was introduced to her this time, the Queen said, "We have met before". You can well imagine the effect of the Queen "remembering" this had on Nellie!

Opticians

In 1948 the Society made arrangements for a qualified optician to attend at the Essex Road premises on the second Wednesday in each week. As this was the first year of the National Health Service, when demand for spectacles shot up because now they were free, this must have been a good move.

Chemists

In 1947 the Co-op chemists claimed to be strategically placed, **nearly** opposite the doctors' surgeries in New Street but they were also not far from the chemist, Kenneth Reed in Queen's Parade, who had claimed to be opposite the surgeries as early as 1936. The chemists, too, found their business growing once the National Health Service was in force.

HCMS P2003.400.250

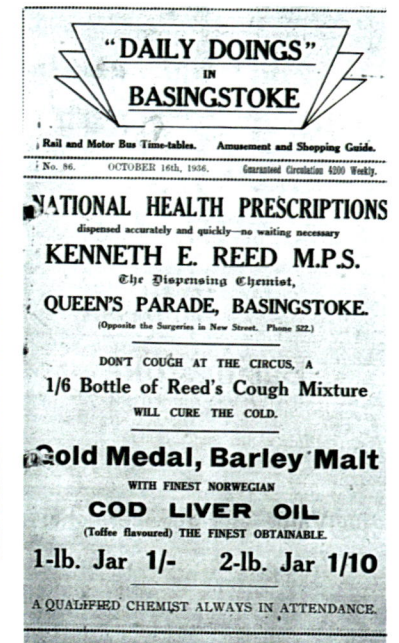

New Drapery Department

A 'BC' D-DAY
Tuesday, 5th December
WHEN WE OPEN OUR
NEW DRAPERY DEPT.
At 18, New St.
AND ASSIST OUR MEMBERS TO ENJOY A HAPPY CHRISTMAS BY RETURNING TO THEM IN
DIVIDEND & INTEREST
OVER £10,000
YOU CAN ALSO OBTAIN...
Value for Money and Guineas for Pounds
by Co-operative Shopping
BASINGSTOKE
CO-OPERATIVE
SOCIETY LIMITED
ESSEX ROAD, BASINGSTOKE

Another shop was opened in New Street in 1950, taking over the premises on the corner of New Street and Winchester Street which had been Clarke & Wells, drapers. The shop shown on the advertisement looks rather grander than any known in New Street, and perhaps it was wishful thinking to show the crowds so great as to need a policeman in control.

HCMS P2005.1726 DPAAOR29

There was a summer sale at these premises in 1955. The footwear Department had its own premises farther down New Street.

WATCH OUR WINDOWS EACH DAY FOR EXCEPTIONAL BARGAINS
Huge Reductions in Drapery, Men's Wear and Footwear Depts

Wherever you were, you could enter this film contest in January 1955. It would be interesting to see the entries and to know who won the electric iron.

Enquire at your nearest Basingstoke Branch
of the
BASINGSTOKE CO-OPERATIVE SOCIETY
for details of the
"FOR BETTER FOR WORSE"
FILM CONTEST
and win a
MORPHY-RICHARDS 'ATLANTIC' ELECTRIC IRON
Lightweight Model

This Morphy Richards electric iron is on display in Milestones Museum.

Oakridge

The Co-op caravan . . .
   Mary Brian

At one time Oakridge Road was not a very long road and it stopped in the middle of nowhere. At the end of that road was an open piece of land that was left specifically for the building of a shop and possibly a pub at the time and maybe another shop; but at the end of that there was a small caravan which was run by the Co-op. In those days I was quite young and I wasn't that interested in shopping for food.

Not long after we moved down from London the shop was built and the Co-op opened it to replace their caravan. It thrived, and it was a really successful shop for years. As the estates grew around it, it seemed to do even better. It was a very good little shop and there was a great deal of camaraderie. People used to go in there not just to shop but to actually talk to one another. There was a lot of friendship that developed there.

South Ham

In 1955 the Co-op opened a new butchery branch for the growing estate of South Ham in King's Road. Another new shop, Groves, newsagent, opened the same day, two doors up. Later the Co-op opened a grocery shop at no 39, which also competed with Groves for the cigarettes and sweets trade. No 41 is now the Hospice Shop.

BASINGSTOKE CO-OPERATIVE SOCIETY LTD.
have pleasure in announcing that their
BUTCHERY BRANCH
at
37 KING'S ROAD SOUTH HAM
will open on
TUESDAY, MARCH 29th

Mr. A. E. Groves
NEWSAGENT
has pleasure in announcing the opening of his shop at
41, KINGS ROAD
on
TUESDAY, MARCH 29th
Also Cigarettes, Tobacco and Sweets

I learned a lot about wine!
   Phyl Millar

When the Co-op in Essex Road closed eventually I went up to King's Road in South Ham, did the checkout, and I used to go on the milk tokens, cigarettes, wine counter - I learned a lot about wine! At King's Road we didn't have to cut up the cheese, or pat the butter, that had already been done.

A range of styles

The second half of the Fifties saw a wider range of goods advertised and a variety of design styles.

Male models now

A cartoon character

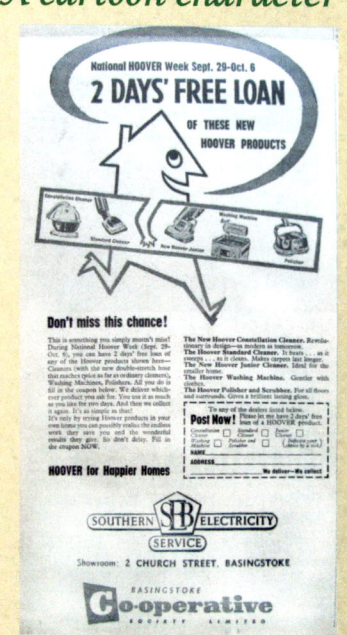

Sarum Hill

The Drill Hall had originally been put up in 1883 by Colonel May, brewer, in the first of his six years as Mayor. He was instrumental in setting up K Company, 1st Hampshire Rifle Volunteers.

The hall is seen here decorated for the May Centenary in 1897, celebrating 100 years in which various members of the May family had been Mayors.

HCMS P2003.400.284.1 DPAA 1097

In 1937 the Drill Hall was converted to be the Plaza cinema (often called "The Fleapit"), with a new frontage.

The small building on the right was the Masonic Hall erected in 1885. Both were often used for Co-op meetings until the Co-op Furnishing Store was opened here in May 1955.

Photo TSC Archives

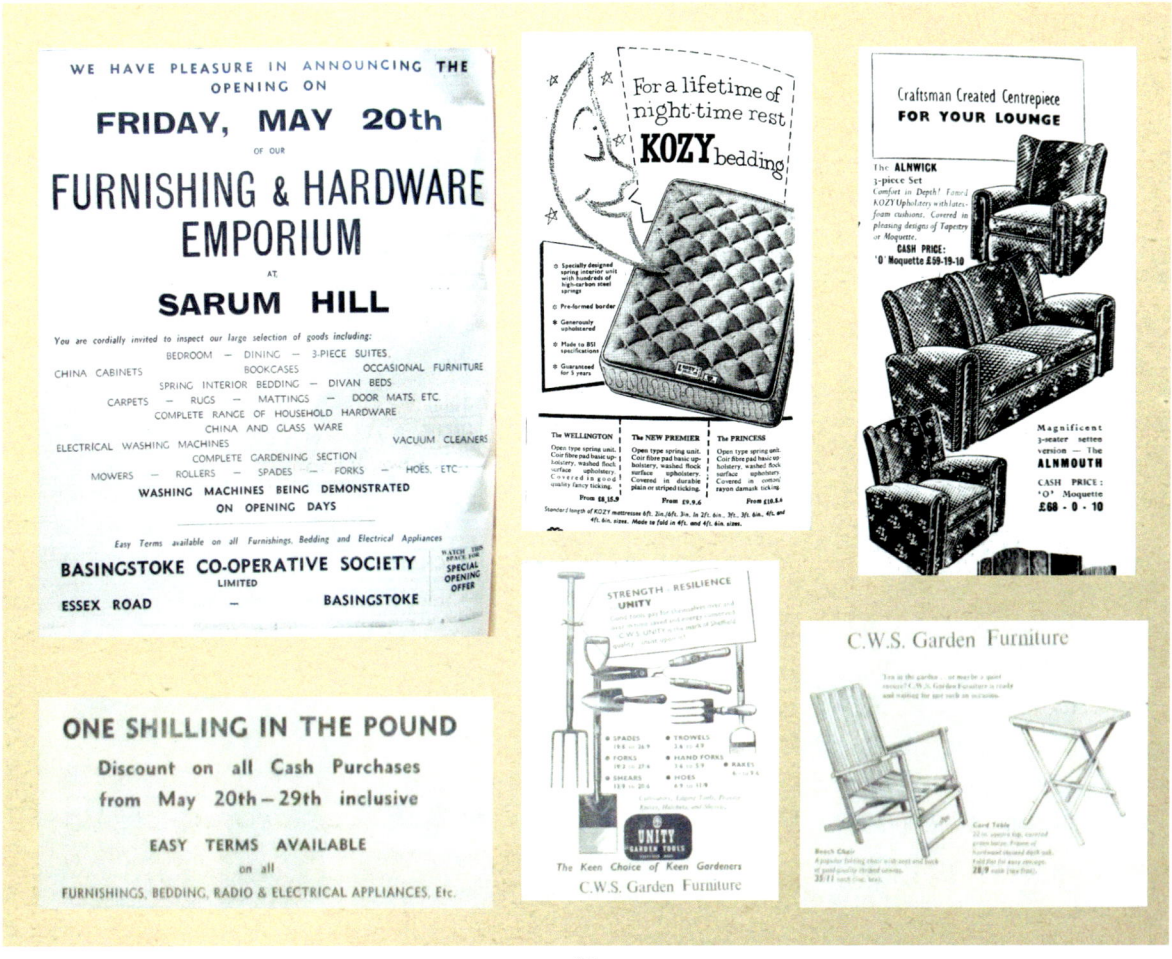

Presentation To Employees, 1954

The first two were made by Mr. C. Butler, vice-chairman of the Management Committee. "I am pleased to be able to say that during the last trading year the sales of the Society expanded at a rate which was only exceeded by one other Society in the Hants and Sussex District and the committee are pleased to acknowledge the large part which the efforts of employees have played in achieving this result.

"I think this would be a good opportunity also to pay tribute to our outside staff, who, in the recent appalling weather, maintained all the Society's services in conditions of some severity."

Mr. Butler then made presentations to Mr. M. Taylor and Mr. B. Brown, two members of the staff who had each completed over 21 years with the Society.

To Mr. Taylor, who is the manager of the New Street butchery department, he presented a fireside chair. To Mr. Brown, who is the dairy foreman, he presented a clock.

Mr. Butler went on, "Mr. Davies, a member of our office staff, has, during the year, achieved a pass in Co-operative Law and Administration. This is Mr. Davies' sixth success in Co-operative Union Examinations." Mr. Butler then presented Mr. Davies with a book token on behalf of the committee.

All the recipients briefly replied after they had received their gifts.

Another presentation, this time on behalf of the employees to Mr. Jack Lintern, was made by Mr. A. Rooms, the former bakery manager. Mr. Rooms paid high tribute to Mr. Lintern's diligence as a baker's roundsman for 27 years with the Society, who never failed to complete a round no matter what the weather. Mr. Lintern was apparently much too shy to express his own thanks, and Mr. Rooms read a letter from him.

HBG 5.3 1954

The Basingstoke Co-operative Society in Kelly's Directory 1958

Essex Road

35-39	Bakers, butchers & grocers
41	Registered office

New Street

11a	Bakers
12	Footwear
13	Chemist
15	Outfitters
16 & 17	Grocers
18	Drapers

Kings Road, South Ham

37 & 39	Butchers and grocers

Soper Grove

37	Grocers and butchers

Oakridge Road

37 & 39	Grocers

Winchester Street

28 & 30	Drapers and butchers

Railway Goods Yard
   Coal depot

HCMS p2005.873 DPAAJMP67

In the choir...
Margaret Hayward

I was a member of the Basingstoke Co-operative Junior Choir. You can see the initials BCJC on the flag. It was a mixed choir of boys and girls, which went on for several years. Mrs Price, the piano teacher, was our choir mistress.

This photograph is of our annual concert in 1950, at the old Queen Mary's School (now The Vyne School). I am on the left in the back row. The girls all wore white blouses and green pinafore dresses.

For a time we rehearsed in a room over the Essex Road shops. We sang in all sorts of places. Sometimes we went out to perform in village halls and at Christmas we used to go around carol singing to old people's homes.

CO-OPERATIVE SOCIETY'S SUPPER DANCE

In 1954 the Management Committee and the Staff Social Club combined to provide a grand supper dance and entertainment at the Town Hall which according to the report in the *Hants & Berks Gazette*, "surpassed all others", with food and drink on "a lavish scale", the food prepared by the catering staff being "distinctly appetising to the palate and delectable to the eye". The managing secretary, Mr H A Toogood, helped the "overtaxed barmen".

Dancing was to Stan Rogers and his Blue Star Players, and entertainment was also provided by two vocalists and a comedian.

Social events

A disaster avoided...
Mary Andrews

Because my husband, Reg, was a milkman for the Co-op when we got married in 1952, we had our wedding reception at the Co-op Restaurant. In those days that was at Winton House, in Winton Square. We had a roast and trifle and it cost 25 shillings a head for about 50 people.

Ernie West, who was the cook from the Co-op bakery in Essex Road, made the 3-tier wedding cake. Unfortunately it was accidentally dropped and the icing cracked but somehow it was mended.

Seeing the clown...
Alan Andrews

I remember as a kid when my father worked in the Co-op down in Essex Road as a milkman, they used to have many more family trips out. I once remember going on a trip to Wembley Arena and seeing a clown that played the saxophone. That stayed in my mind, I probably was 8 or 9 years old at the time.

The Co-op had its own Cricket Club.

Basingstoke Co-operative Society Cricket Club, who played in the Memorial Park last week.

You had a good time.
Joan Hobbs

> The Co-op had a Social Club and they used to have a Co-op Social at the Town Hall every year. It was very nice. We used to go up there in the afternoon and blow up balloons and decorate it and then we'd have this Co-op Social in the evening. The Town Hall was a nice place to have it because it's got a very elegant staircase and you feel quite posh when you come, all dressed up coming down these stairs. We had a dance - waltzes, and quicksteps, and Palais glides - and they used to have some refreshments and you had a good time because you mixed with people that you worked with and you knew most of them.

Women's Co-operative Guild

In April 1959 the Guild held a party in the Labour Hall to celebrate their 60th birthday. Miss Piila, the acting secretary of the International Guild, who came from Finland, said there were 22 guilds in existence.

Mrs E M Springall, presiding, received the Rainbow Flag from Mrs A Ward.

At the conclusion of the tea an iced cake, given by the Federation's bakery at Guildford, was cut by Mrs A Graddon and Mrs F M Kelly, who had both served 25 years with the Guild.

A new Store for an expanding town

NEW CO-OP BUILDING WILL BE MOST MODERN IN BASINGSTOKE

In March 1959 the *Hants & Berks Gazette* announced that the Borough Development subcommittee had approved a plan for the erection of new shop premises at the junction of Winchester Street and New Street. At this point discussions were underway for an agreement to be made with the London County Council for a deliberate, planned expansion of the town to accommodate "London overspill". This was not yet the tripartite agreement that was eventually reached in 1961 between the Basingstoke Borough Council, the Hampshire County Council and the London County Council, which would provide for the construction of 11,500 dwellings for an estimated overspill population of 36,800. Even so, a statement from the Basingstoke Co-operative Society said that they "intended to provide shopping facilities more in keeping with the increased population which is expected during the next few years". They had made their plans before the LCC agreement and had decided to provide the new shop now, rather than wait till still more people had actually arrived in the town.

It is a sign of the times too that in 1959 the Borough Council approved a block of 38 garages at Jordans Nurseries in Winchester Road, Kelmscot Building Company were given approval for 32 pairs of semi-detached houses in the western extension of the Harrow Way Estate, and an application by A J Sapp and Son to build offices, stores and garages in Southern Road was deferred, while Blue Peter Retreads were refused permission to erect an office block at 396 Worting Road, as this would be out of keeping with the residential area.

In October 1959, the same month the agreement with the LCC was signed, the *Hants & Berks Gazette* carried an article about the new Co-op building, with a photograph of the model. They announced that "A £200,000 multi-store for Basingstoke Co-operative Society, selling everything from clothes to pork chops, and from indigestion tablets to hardware, may well set the tone for the Basingstoke of the future".

> Providing 226ft of glass windows extending from the Post Office in New Street to the extent of their premises in Winchester Street, the new store will be the first major step towards a bright modern shopping centre for the town.
>
> It will replace a whole string of small shops which the Co-op has bought up over the years and occupied until a scheme of this type could be launched, and the whole building will be set back fifteen feet. This will allow wider roads and end the notorious New Street traffic jams.
>
> The new Co-op will have no present rivals to the title of the most striking building in Basingstoke. Of two storeys, including offices, and a lift, it will have a main entrance near its centre with a smaller one at each end.
>
> It extends backwards considerably and will have a total area of 22,000 feet super, and the designers have provided for the addition of a third storey atop the other two should the future needs demand it.
>
> Although of ultra modern clean exterior appearance the store will be a conventional structure with brick as the main material. Inside, everything will be as pleasant and attractive as modern designers can make it.

HBG 16.10.1959

Although the new premises would come "within a short distance of the existing furniture emporium in Sarum Hill", there were no plans to link the two. The premises in Essex Road would remain in use but "all the offices which are used by members and members of the public will be accommodated in the new building".

Work had already started on demolishing the old shops and it was hoped that the new store would be completed within 16 to 18 months.

The Co-op also demolished this shop, next to the Post Office in New Street, which they had bought in 1958 from Antonio Dellafera, whose wife had carried on an antiques business there. Before that it had been owned by the Postmaster General (the Post Office was next door) and before that it had been known as New Street House, owned by Charles Webb, who died in 1875, and then by Charles Frere Webb, surgeon, who added more property on the south side and died in 1911. Oddly enough, its main entrance was not on New Street itself but at the side.

HBG 16.10.1959

So the 1950s ended with demolition and dust . . .

HCMS DPAAMP63 and 64

. . . and with advertisements for Christmas and a cheery message.

THE SIXTIES

... Population 25980 (1961) ... London overspill agreement (1964) ...

Before the new Stores opened

In the first year of the Sixties the *Hants & Berks Gazette* had a Co-op advertisement every week, usually on page 8. They showed much the same mixture of goods as in previous years. For men there were jackets, shirts, and ties, "Society suits" and underwear, as well as "clothes for craftsmen", perhaps ushering in the age of DIY. There was underwear for ladies too, corsetry for the fuller figure and a floral cotton dress. Shoes ranged from children's sandals and "Skip-along shoes" to stilettos. Many of the clothes shown in these advertisements looked familiar, repeating styles from previous years.

South Ham

A duster in your hand...
Hazel Lysaght

> I was just 15 when I went to work at the Co-op in King's Road. We were issued with heavily starched overalls, which we wore at all times. Shops were just becoming self service but pre-packed goods had not become the norm, there were still a lot of things that had to be weighed and packed in the warehouse at the back of the shop, such as all the dried fruit (glacé cherries were the worst to handle), dry goods such as lentils, dried pulses and rice, all of these things had to be removed from the shelves each week and the weight checked, the weight could vary according to the humidity.
>
> Cheese and bacon also had to be prepared in the warehouse, the whole cheeses had to be skinned, some of the skins came off easily but some of them were as tough as old boots, the best piece of the cheese was the square from the middle. The sides of bacon had to be boned, jointed and sliced into rashers, the bacon slicer was a vicious machine that had to be cleaned down at the end of each day, or when it was to be used for cold meats; this was the domain of the Provisions Manager.
>
> Each week there was a delivery and then anybody that was not working on the tills was expected to help unload the lorry and carry the goods into the warehouse (it kept one fit).
>
> We were expected to be seen to be busy at all times, the Manager had a small office in the warehouse, with a window at the back of the shop, which he would tap on if he thought you were idling about. So you always made sure you had a duster in your hand if he was around.

Stock checking was done once a year and had to be done after hours and on Sunday; if there were any discrepancies it was repeated monthly until the stock was correct. One year stocks were wrong because one of the women had been helping herself. We worked Monday until Saturday with half day closing on Thursday. There was a summer outing to the seaside and a Christmas party at the Town Hall each year. During my time at the Co-op I worked with some very nice people and got to know a lot of the customers.

Sawdust on the floor . . .
Lynne Cooper

I think I was about seven or eight years old at the time, so we are looking at around 1961-62, when my Mum asked me to go up to the Co-op in King's Road, South Ham. I had to get 2s 6d worth of minced meat that would feed a family of five.

So I walked up to the shops, stopping along the way to hang upside-down on the metal bars that ran around the outside of King's Road Playing Field. Those same bars with the cement posts with their 'ice-cream' tops are still there today and still bring a smile to my face as I remember how, as children, my sister and I used to take our dolls up there and give them a swing or a slide down the huge slide. When we went down we nearly always ended up shooting off the end as somebody had polished the metal part so they could go faster down it.

Anyway, after the little detour of the playing fields, I ended up at the Co-op Butchers, which at that time was quite separate from the Co-op Stores. And as I waited for the man to prepare the mince I can remember all the sawdust on the floor of the shop and can recall drawing patterns in it with my feet.

Winklebury

The Co-op van . . .
Pauline Dolan

I came to Basingstoke in 1960 when the Clarke Estate was being built. I lived in Wellington Terrace and later moved to Dunsford Crescent and, like all the neighbours, I used to walk to the "Co-op van", a kind of permanent Portakabin. There was usually only one man serving. I remember going up its steps, perhaps to be handed something like a tin of peas but they didn't have much stock there. Mostly you collected and paid for milk tokens that you put out each day so that the milkman would know how many bottles to leave. I had an order book and used to write in it what I wanted and hand it in at the van and then the groceries would be delivered from the main Co-op.

Wellington Terrace and Dunsford Crescent were owned by Park Prewett and had been built for their staff - not just nursing staff but gardeners and farm people. I didn't only shop at the Co-op. I used to walk into town a couple of times a week with one child in the pram and one on the baby seat - walking down Kingsclere Road past fields where we picked mushrooms. I might buy some groceries at Ody's at the top of the town and put them on the basket under the pram.

The 1968 Kelly's Directory recorded the Basingstoke Co-operative Society Ltd, grocers, and a parade of shops on Elmswood Parade on the south side of Elmswood Way, next to the Wellington Social Club set up for staff at Park Prewett Hospital. There was also a Post Office in Roman Road.

The January Sale notice the following year showed customers hurrying for bargains. There was a Sale too in the furniture and furnishings department at Sarum Hill. The fitting out of all the departments in Co-operative House was a lengthy job, and In 1963 it was announced that the programme would be completed early the following year.

On Television!

The new store attracted media attention.

JANUARY SALE

Starts WEDNESDAY, 10th Jan.
BARGAINS in
DRAPERY, MEN'S WEAR, FOOTWEAR.
COME EARLY TO BEAT THE RUSH

BASINGSTOKE
Co-operative
SOCIETY LIMITED

I.T.V. Commercial Being Filmed At Basingstoke

CO-OPERATIVE HOUSE WILL BE THE SCENE OF ATTRACTION ON TUESDAY DECEMBER 10

Tuesday will mark the first of a series of ITV Commercial Break features for release in 1964. The C.W.S. Publicity Department in conjunction with the film company have selected Co-operative House from a large number of societies in the south, to play this important role.

Highlighted next week will be Wheatsheaf Bread for promotion in the Come Co-operative Shopping Campaign. This section, which has recently been modernised, has attracted considerable attention. Since being resited and refixtured it has recorded considerable trade increases, now in excess of 60 per cent.

Congratulations must be extended to all members of the staff and the C.W.S. Bakery Division in the promotion of this successful experiment.

The next in the series of films to be produced will be recorded in the Food Hall, Co-operative House, New Street, and will use as its theme, "a shopper with a basket."

Co-operative House is adopting a new look with improved departments and sections. At present half of the programme has been completed covering the Fashions, electrical, footwear, Stationery, and confectionery Departments.

Early in the new year we will see the completion of this programme, in which attention will be given to the Fancy glass and China, Hardware and Kitchen utensils, and improved Office counter facilities.

Why not when in town, visit our "new look" store?

HBG6.12.1963

"The Great Day"

OPENING CELEBRATION – MONDAY, NOVEMBER 27th, at 11.30 a.m.

Our *Wonderful* New Promenade Store Co-operative House

OUR NEW PROMENADE STORE

The exploded view shows you where every department is to be found . . . how you can PROMENADE from one department to the next . . . from the FOOD HALL, complete with greengrocery stall and confectionery counter, into the butchery . . . up the main staircase, through men's outwear, children's wear, into the richly carpeted fashion salon!

WORTH A BUS RIDE TO SEE

Worth a bus ride to shop there too! Promenade shopping is so easy! Start with the pharmacy for your cosmetic or chemist shopping (prescriptions are dispensed in the modern dispensary attached).

Walk through into the drapery, then into men's underwear. Just behind: the shoe section, with smart new chairs to try on that pair of Fashion shoes.

Ascend the staircase to the magnificent Fashion Salon, soft carpet underfoot, and all the latest fashions to see.

On the first floor too (there is a lift up to it also), men's and teenage outerwear, baby linen, and the complete electrical department—moved from Sarum Hill.

Back on the ground floor and into the splendid Food Hall. Every possible grocery need is within reach for self service. On the way out you will see the greengrocery stall, and confectionery counter—with freshly baked Wheatsheaf bread every day, and a wonderful choice of cakes.

Step straight out of the Food Hall into the butchery! Pale blue tiles show up the game and poultry, besides carcass meat hanging there. Below are chilled display counters for bacon, sausages, canned meats, etc. Every week there is a speciality. It may be pork, Aberdeen Angus Scotch Beef or game.

Yes, it's worth a bus fare to shop in Co-operative House!

The opening of Co-operative House at the end of 1961 was a big event for the town and the *Hants & Berks Gazette* did it proud.

This was a two-storey building of steel frame structure with pre-cast concrete floors. It had been designed so that another floor could be added to cater for future expansion. There was electrical floor heating throughout, and flush lighting fitted into the ceilings. Outside, a raised canopy round the length of the building provided protection for shoppers.

Mr Thirlwall, the managing secretary of the Basingstoke Society, said that the stores employed approximately seventy people.

The exploded view shows you where every department is to be found . . . how you can PROMENADE from one department to the next . . . from the FOOD HALL, complete with greengrocery stall and confectionery counter, into the butchery . . . up the main staircase, through men's outwear, children's wear, into the richly carpeted fashion salon!

HBG 1.12.1961

Fashions and Foundations

The *Hants & Berks Gazette* report included photos of some departments that were already open.

Trying on the hats . . .
Joan Hobbs

In 1964-5 I took a part time job in the Fashion Department of the Co-op. My task was to assist Mrs Maisie Butler (later to become Mrs Wilkinson) on the Accessories Counter. This covered hats as well as scarves and gloves and many laughs were shared as we helped customers to select their purchases.

Quite often, when customers were few, we would rather naughtily try on all the hats from the display. These hats ranged from the frankly frumpish to delicious confections suitable for weddings and many hilarious moments were spent away from our counter while we paraded in varieties of headgear.

The whole department was presided over by Mrs Rocca and I also recall two charming window dressers called Mary and Veronica. Other names remembered are Mrs Pengelly in Fashions and Mrs May and her willing young assistant Pat, who greatly enjoyed their jobs in Baby Linen.

Our Manager was Mr Harold Watson, who was also a stalwart member of All Saints Church. I believe he and his wife retired to Devon.

On one of my Saturdays, I popped down to the Chemist's Shop during my lunch break and very mistakenly helped myself to a long squirt of what turned out to be a particularly obnoxious perfume. I was unable to get rid of it as a large proportion of the stuff had soaked into my clothes. My return to the counter was met by my workmates fanning the air for relief! No-one could bear to stand close to me and for the rest of the afternoon the Accessories counter smelled like an Eastern Bazaar.

Everything was available.
   Margaret Hayward

> I liked the new stores. You used to be able to go there and buy your shoes, buy your clothes, buy your linen, everything was available.

Menswear

Shoes

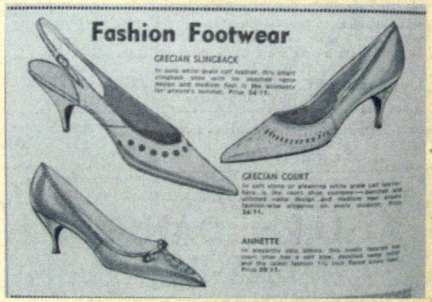

Groceries

The second half of 1963 saw an increasing number of adverts in the *Hants & Berks Gazette*.

In July there were two adverts for a Sale, advising customers to "WATCH OUR WINDOWS" and "SHOP EARLY", while there were Special Offers that month and in August and October.

Compare the self-service basket shown in August with the popular "gondola basket" of October.

In September there was "the biggest ever Australian Food Festival" at Co-operative House "and at all our 19 grocery branches". If emigrating to Australia wasn't possible, the fall-back position was buying their fruit.

COME CO-OPERATIVE SHOPPING FOR BAGS OF AUSTRALIAN SUNSHINE

AND SAVE ON THESE SPECIAL OFFERS

WHEATSHEAF AUSTRALIAN CHOICE
PEARS 2/4   PEACHES HALVES AND SLICES 2/3
WHEATSHEAF PURE DAIRY CREAM 1/1½   11d Delicious with Australian Fruit
CRUMPSALL CREAM CRACKERS 1/-   10d Perfect with Australian Butter and Cheese
SUNSIP & FRUIT SQUASHES 2/3 2/4 plus 3d bottle deposit

There were no advertisements for the butchery department. But there were tempting goods in the new showroom. Finance offers too.

VISIT OUR NEW CHINA, GLASS AND CUTLERY SHOWROOM
NOW ON THE GROUND FLOOR AT CO-OPERATIVE HOUSE

Windsor Bone China

Come Co-operative Shopping
gifts for the home...

BASINGSTOKE CO-OPERATIVE SOCIETY LTD.

Invest in our DEVELOPMENT BONDS earning interest at

5% Per Annum

MINIMUM DEPOSIT £10

For further particulars apply to:
Managing Secretary
Basingstoke Co-operative Society Ltd.
Co-operative House, New Street, Basingstoke

BASINGSTOKE CO-OPERATIVE FURNISHING DEPARTMENT
SARUM HILL
THE SHOP WITH THE BIGGEST SELECTION IN TOWN TO OFFER

WE STOCK, OR CAN OBTAIN, ALL THE LEADING MAKES OF FURNITURE, BEDROOM SUITES, DINING SETS, THREE-PIECES, STUDIO COUCHES, CARPETS, RUGS, ETC.
● PRICES ARE STRICTLY COMPETITIVE
● A PERSONAL SERVICE IS OUR AIM

Sarum Hill was still the place for carpets, furniture, pots and pans.

CO-OPERATIVE CARPET EVENT
FRIDAY, MAY 10TH, TO SATURDAY, MAY 18TH
PLUS DIVIDEND   H.P. TERMS AVAILABLE

EXAMPLES

ALL WELL KNOWN MAKES - GUARANTEED

*

SPECIAL OFFER
BROADLOOM CARPET

Good Quality Underfelt HALF PRICE
RUGS — ASSORTED SIZES AT REDUCED PRICES
INLAID LINO FROM 15/6 TO 10/8 SQUARE YARD
FLOOR COVERING FROM 3/6 TO 2/11 SQUARE YARD

BASINGSTOKE CO-OPERATIVE SOCIETY Ltd
FURNISHING DEPARTMENT   SARUM HILL

CARPETS
The best selection, quality, value!

Be ready for the sun and the summer!
DECK CHAIRS BY SOCIETY
19/11
CLUB CHAIRS

You'll smile when your friends cast envious glances...

Such a compliment to your sound furnishing sense. You'll be glad you bought a SOCIETY suite, and will smile when you think how **little it cost**

The 'Garsdale' suite—designed in traditional style, has a 4'6" Sideboard, draw leaf table and four chairs with padded seats. Beautiful oak finish. A suite you'll be proud to own for only **£48-12-6**
Alternative gate leg table and 4'6" Sideboard available if preferred, at a little extra cost.

Available on the easiest of H.P. Terms

Society FURNITURE is made to last
Basingstoke **Co-operative** SOCIETY LIMITED

Like a second family . . .
Alan Andrews

I started work at the Co-op furnishing store in Sarum Hill in 1967 when I was 15. I remember my first weekly wage packet, £5 10s. I thought I was really rich. I also remember that it was the first time I'd ever used a telephone and I found that quite daunting. I also found that my schoolwork, particularly my spelling, wasn't that good, so I had to find a telephone directory and a local map of the town to find out how to spell all these words, because it was quite embarrassing when I first started.

The first year you couldn't serve a customer on your own at all, you were supervised with anything, you weren't allowed near a till. It was like a big family, but quite strict for somebody of my age being in there.

It was a great place to work. The staff were all very good people. Mr John Cooper was the manager and the deputy manager was Jean Kopolweski, better known as Mr Koppy. Mr Koppy did things so precisely, back in the days before sellotape when we used to wrap up parcels with the old brown paper & string and he'd spend ages on just one parcel and it would be absolutely immaculate. Other people there were Roy Campbell, Mary Kearney, Ella Wason and Mrs Wiley. We also had a delivery team, Mr Jack Rutt and Mr Tubby Bond, better known - fondly known as Laurel and Hardy. And if you saw them you'd know why!

I was the youngest there when I started at 15. It was only going to be temporary, I was going to go back to apprenticeships but that didn't materialise, so I stayed and learned re-upholstery, French polishing, just about everything that needed doing I ended up doing. I eventually passed my driving test and then we started getting people wanting fitted carpets. As I was the only one that could drive, "Alan, you can go and do the measuring." And that's really how I got into the carpet side of the business.

In the store we sold all sorts of furniture - beds, even garden furniture, lawn mowers, kitchen furniture - we seemed to sell everything in there at one time or another. In latter years we went on to see staff changes. Vera Cubitt, Peter Godfrey, Nobby Clarke. We also had delivery drivers, I remember Paul Bosley, David Bedford and Joe Wason. And we started to have Saturday boys, I remember Kevin Vickery and Adrian Daly.

Before my time the building had been used as a cinema and underneath, where people couldn't see, was still the old slope to the original stage. We also had the oldest gas boiler in Basingstoke. It was so big you could actually get inside it. We used to have a good laugh when the British Gas people used to come to inspect and clean it and said they'd never seen anything like it - and in fact at the end we only had one chap in the Basingstoke vicinity that would even look at it. That was, you know, something to see, but eventually it packed up, we couldn't get the spare parts so they had to have another boiler put in.

Opening times were 8.30 to 5.30 Monday to Saturday, with half day closing on Thursdays at one o'clock, I used to enjoy half days.

I remember old prices - I recently went to a customer in Sherborne St John who was my first whole house, furniture and carpet and accessories, and I had a great time looking at invoices that I'd written 30-odd years ago - and the prices. Top quality Axminster carpet, £4 17 6d a square yard. Four foot six bed and head board, £14 10s. A three-piece suite £59. Or a top quality Oxer Upholstery Basingstoke made suite for 99 guineas - never sold a lot of those! Men used to come into the store on a Friday afternoon to tell us that they were coming in with their wife on Saturday, maybe to buy a suite, and that they wouldn't be prepared to pay more than £150 and not to show their wife anything dearer than that. And we used to greet them on the Saturday as if we hadn't seen them for months.

At Christmas, after closing time, we used to have a few drinks and snacks in the shop, but there wasn't a staff Christmas party as such.

The Electrical Department was now in New Street, and the chemist's was still in Winchester Street. The chemist's was now selling cameras and films, even cine cameras.

Soper Grove

The Directors' report for the half year ended 28th September 1963 described work on the premises in Soper Grove, north of the railway.

> SOPER GROVE
> The economical conversion of the separate grocery and butchery shops into a single unit has been completed and made possible a complete revision of the interior layout. Increasing trade at the branch has justified the changes made.

Off-licences

Off-licences were becoming popular. The Directors' report for the half-year ended 4th April 1964 described a move from Aldermaston to Tadley and an attempt was made to get an off-licence in Oakridge.

> OFF-LICENCE
>
> The Off-Licence business, formerly carried on from our branch at Aldermaston, has now been transferred to Franklin Avenue, Tadley, where it is more conveniently situated for the majority of Members in that area.

A Witness in Court . . .
Mary Brian

The Co-op at Oakridge wanted to apply for a drinks licence. At that time Mr Rapson in Vyne Road had the only shop in the town where you could buy alcohol, an off-licence, and he objected and I think other shops objected as well. So the Co-op had to go to court. And because she was a member of the Co-op Women's Guild, my sister had to go to court as a witness to say it would be a good thing for the community that they could go and buy drinks. But when she was interviewed by the lawyer employed by the other shops, he really shredded her, he gave her a really hard time and she was made to feel as if she was an alcoholic who couldn't wait to get down town to buy her drinks! But nevertheless the Co-op did actually get their drinks licence.

Dividend Stamps

In 1966 the Co-op introduced a National Dividend Stamp Scheme as a new way of distributing the "Divi". A colourful booklet invited members to endorse the scheme - which they did.

Advantages for the customer

Speedy redemption more appealing
Customers will know that a full stamp book can be exchanged for cash or goods or invested immediately.

More convenient
Customers will not need to make a special trip to 'draw dividend'.

New customers can benefit easily
New customers will benefit immediately from Co-op Dividend Stamps. They will be encouraged to shop at the Co-op regularly – and to join the Society for its additional benefits.

More pleasure in shopping
Stamps have an irresistible appeal. Collecting stamps adds pleasure and excitement to modern shopping.
(And the stamps are an ever-present reminder to "come again".)

More pleasure in shopping

The Co-operative Women's Guild

The banner of the Basingstoke Branch is hand-embroidered on corded cotton. It has the earlier title of "Women's Co-operative Guild" as well as "Basingstoke Branch". The white rose is the symbol of the southern section of the Co-operative Society while the ears of wheat are the symbol of the Co-operative Movement.

The Committee Minutes of 17th May 1962 report that Mrs Smith was in attendance with the banner but this was obviously not yet complete, as "the Secy was requested to write to H.O. to see if information could be obtained regarding the date of opening of our Branch. Mrs Smith felt that this date should be on the banner."

When it was hung for the first time, Mrs Miller, as secretary, wrote, "It did our hearts good to see at last the banner that had been so long talked of."

The 1960s were a busy time for the Guild. They made visits to various Co-op factories: the bakery at Fareham, the Laundry and the Ideal Clothiers in Wellingborough. At the Harlow biscuit factory they were given a big box of biscuits, so they went back the next year. A report of one of these visits explains, "Members were able to study a different system of Co-operative organisation—Co-operative partnership, where the workers are part-owners of their factory." The following year a member of the headquarters Education Committee came to give a talk on "The Regional Plan—the necessity of the smaller shops to amalgamate in these days of fierce competition". "Members were urged to look ahead to the development of regional societies and to consider the advantages of large scale organisation within the movement."

Bring and Buy — **EVENTS** — *Harvest Sale*

Proceeds to Leprosy Association   Proceeds to Cancer Research Fund

Garden Party, with competition for home-made hats of crepe paper

Competition: The prettiest piece of china or pottery

TALKS BY	TALKS ON
A Health visitor	A Leper hospital in Uganda
A Retired Yeoman Warder	A Woman's Day in the USSR
A Footwear Buyer for PIMCO	The Sports Centre now under construction
Reading Magistrate	Emergencies in the Home

Donations were given to the Cancer Research Fund, the Leprosy Association, the Winston Churchill Memorial Fund and the Oxfam Bechuanaland project, as well as toys to the Save the Children Fund.

In 1966 it was reported that members had assisted organisations in the town: Oxfam, Park Prewett League of Friends, Red Cross Flag Day, Old People's Welfare, Basingstoke Joint Women's Association coffee morning, Mentally Handicapped, Life and Action for the Crippled child and the Mayor's walk in aid of the new Sports Centre.

The Secretary kept a scrapbook of photos of outings and social events and regularly sent reports of their activities to the *Basingstoke Gazette*.:

MY HOLIDAY — IT WAS HILARIOUS!

'BAN THESE TOYS' CALL

The Guild had a display at an exhibition at Winklebury, where their banner was much in evidence. Mrs Miller, the secretary, was on the left and Mrs Smith, who had made the banner, was on the right.

Documents about the Basingstoke branch of the Co-operative Women's Guild consulted at the Portsmouth Record Office:
Minutes books and report books 1929-1978
1603A/4/5/1-13 and /15
Scrapbook 1964-68 *1603A/4/5/14*

The archives of the Basingstoke Co-operative Women's Guild, held in Portsmouth Record Office, include the programme, adjudication and adjudicator's comments on their entry for the 1969 Drama Festival. They had got third prize in 1966 but nothing in 1967 and 1968 - perhaps they had been too busy campaigning on various matters to rehearse.

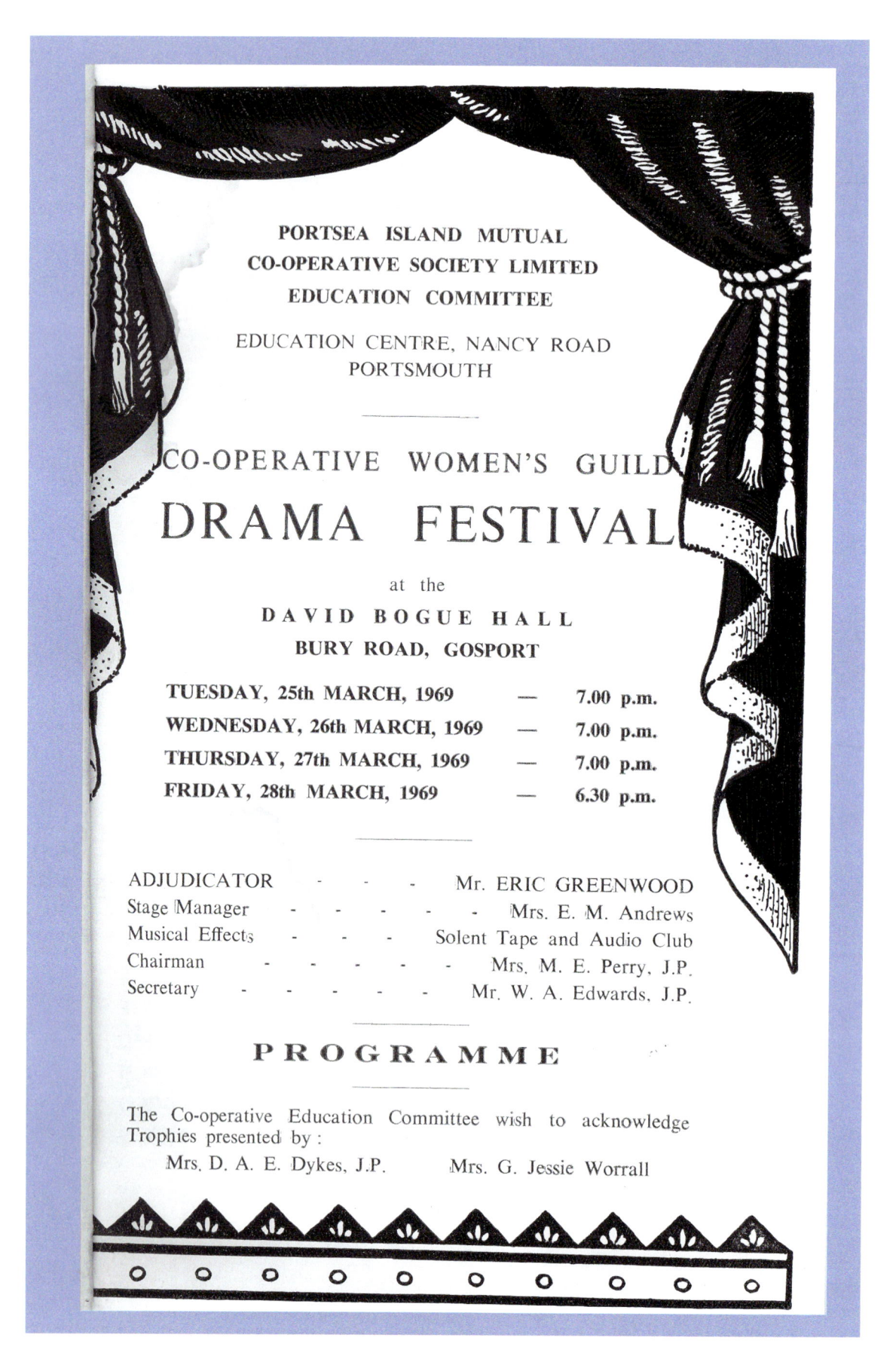

**PORTSEA ISLAND MUTUAL
CO-OPERATIVE SOCIETY LIMITED
EDUCATION COMMITTEE**

EDUCATION CENTRE, NANCY ROAD
PORTSMOUTH

CO-OPERATIVE WOMEN'S GUILD

DRAMA FESTIVAL

at the

DAVID BOGUE HALL
BURY ROAD, GOSPORT

TUESDAY, 25th MARCH, 1969	7.00 p.m.
WEDNESDAY, 26th MARCH, 1969	7.00 p.m.
THURSDAY, 27th MARCH, 1969	7.00 p.m.
FRIDAY, 28th MARCH, 1969	6.30 p.m.

ADJUDICATOR	Mr. ERIC GREENWOOD
Stage Manager	Mrs. E. M. Andrews
Musical Effects	Solent Tape and Audio Club
Chairman	Mrs. M. E. Perry, J.P.
Secretary	Mr. W. A. Edwards, J.P.

PROGRAMME

The Co-operative Education Committee wish to acknowledge Trophies presented by :
Mrs. D. A. E. Dykes, J.P.   Mrs. G. Jessie Worrall

WEDNESDAY, 26th MARCH, 1969 — 7.00 p.m.

"PROOF OF THE PUDDING"

by Peter Assinder

Presented by : Basingstoke Branch Co-operative Women's Guild

Producer - DOROTHY JOHNSTONE

Miss Willow (Authoress)	DOROTHY JOHNSTONE
Mona Weede (Secretary)	ELSIE SIMMONDS
Mrs. Martha Brown (Cook)	THERESA OLIVER
Miss Connaught (Director)	PHEBE MILLER
Mrs. Beresford (Chairman)	IVY PARSONS
Fanny Bocock (Martha's Friend)	IRENE CHANDLER

Scene : The Drawing Room of Lavender Lodge. Late Summer.

Time : The Present.

Mrs Phebe Miller, seated on the right, was Secretary of the Basingstoke branch for many years.

ADJUDICATION

GROUP	Basingstoke Branch
PLAY	Proof of the Pudding by Peter Assinder
PRODUCER	Dorothy Johnstone
MARKS	70/100

PRESENTATION 6/10
Care must be taken when positioning furniture, it was all too far down, the performers were above it all the time. Tables "square on" are not conducive to attractive stage pictures and good grouping. "My Lonely Heart" should have been a hard backed book, it would never have sold enough to make a "Paper Back" edition.

PRODUCTION 25/35
The cast tended to play upstage too much, bring them down a bit more, good use was made of the width of the stage. Do watch "scissors" moves, also anticipate entrances and exits, move people to the doors just before the last lines so that they can get off stage quickly. By moving people on their lines, pace can be kept up; the play was well thought out and the cast worked well together.

ACTING 28/40
A very nice characterisation from MISS WILLOW, she looked splendid and her gestures and timing were good. We could have done with a little more volume at times, and the comedy lines needed more pointing to get the full humour. As her secretary, MONA WEEDE could have been a little more distinct, we tended to lose the adenoids in the general inarticulation. Nevertheless it was a credible performance, and there was no need for her appearance of relief on her exits. Another good characterisation came from MRS. BROWN, she looked well and spoke up nicely, her picking up of cues could be tidied up, and she must watch her transition from one mood to another. MISS CONNAUGHT and MRS. BERESFORD both were convincing and nicely audible, they were composed when not actually doing anything and they kept involved. FANNY BOCOCK did very well with an awkward part, we could hear her distinctly, and when she forgot herself and took her hands out of her pockets her acting was good.

ENDEAVOUR 9/15
Had pace been faster this would have been very good entertainment, it was a good choice of play and the whole thing came off quite well.

SUMMING-UP
A play of this type - comedy interspersed with more serious matter needs a light but firm touch. We laughed a lot, but I felt the pace was a little too slow, production was a little scrappy in places.

(signed) ERIC GREENWOOD

Social and international concerns

In 1964 three Basingstoke women won a competition organised by the Guild "to successfully plan their household budgets for two people on less than £3 a week." After complaints that this was not possible, they later explained that this sum only covered meals, not a full household budget.

The Guild made their feelings felt about the affairs of the Basingstoke Co-operative Society itself. In 1967 a suggestion was made by Mrs West that perhaps at a later date the Guild could put forward a proposal that if a third storey was added to the New Street building a restaurant could be incorporated. "This to be borne in mind."

The Guild put forward representations on a range of local and international problems: They were concerned about torture in South Africa and the problems of apartheid. They sent £1 5s for medical aid to Vietnam. Closer to home, they asked the government to ban the production and import of dangerous toys, they called on the government to provide nursery schools with trained staff and they were worried about the plight of elderly people living in old hospitals. They felt the local hospital too needed help.

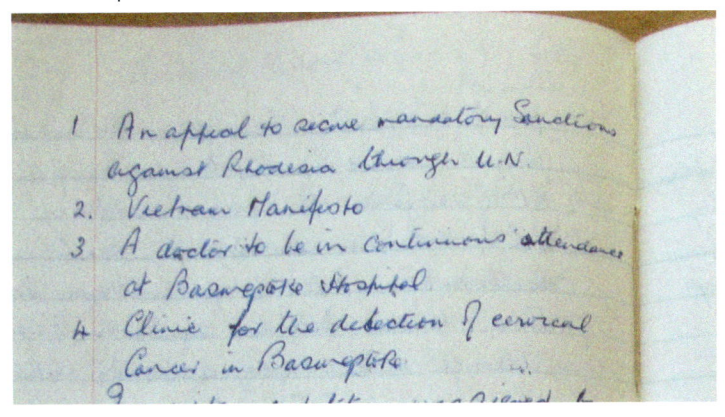

A grateful patient . . .
   Mary Brian

> We came down from London, and of course we were spoilt because we had hospitals, doctors round the corner and everything was there, and swimming pools and goodness knows what, and we found it was very strange that the little local Cottage Hospital didn't have a doctor there all the time. If you needed a doctor they'd phone for one to come in. And I myself remember breaking my ankle on a Saturday, and going up to the hospital and they strapped it up and said ,"Come back on Tuesday because that's when we do X-rays". And so I didn't even know I'd broken my ankle until Tuesday. So that's how old-fashioned it was really, it wasn't that people were bad or anything, it was a good hospital, but they were so behind the times. There was a big campaign by the Co-op Guild and I think the Women's Section of the Labour Party, and they all put pressure on to get something done about this. And I think the combined pressure of those organisations did have quite a good effect because we ended up with a much better service.

An Evening Branch of the Guild

January 25th 1968 saw the inaugural meeting of the Evening Branch, the first new Branch introduced in Basingstoke since 1898, which it was felt "will do much to combat the loneliness of newcomers in the Oakridge area".

Politics

The CWS had debated possible links with the Labour Party in 1927 but at that stage decided against. However, the question of politics came up again many years later with the inauguration of a Voluntary Co-operative Party, Basingstoke in the Labour Hall, Essex Road on 7th November, 1960. The Labour Hall was next to the Co-op premises. It is significant that the seconder of the resolution to form the party was Mrs Springall, chairman of Basingstoke's branch of the Women's Co-operative Guild and Mrs Phebe Miller, who offered the use of a room in her house for meetings, was its secretary, That house can be seen in the photograph on page34 (with the side wall and bay window).

[Handwritten note]: The Isle of Wight Mrs. Higman stated that Basingstoke and Andover were the only towns in her area without a party. Mr. Cornillie presented strong arguments for the formation of a party in Basingstoke. The chairman moved from the chair that a Voluntary Co-operative Party be formed in Basingstoke and the resolution being seconded by Mrs. Springall was unanimously carried.

Some of the themes discussed at meetings were the Co-operative Party Policy Statement "Social Ownership and Control" and the Independent Commission's Report relating to the functions of a Retail Co-operative Society director, when "an interesting discussion ensued". Money held was deposited as share capital under a membership number with the Basingstoke Co-operative Society.

PIMCO

The big event in 1967 was the incorporation of the Basingstoke Co-operative Society into PIMCO (The Portsea Island Mutual Co-operative Society). The Co-operative Women's Guild called a special meeting to consider this but felt it was not sufficiently well advertised and "the small attendance did not represent the membership of our society," so they called another special meeting, well attended this time, which voted by an overwhelming majority for the motion put forward by the board of directors.

The cumbersome title of the new parent, misleadingly suggesting rather a narrow area of interest, was usually shortened to PIMCO. It already had branches at Gosport, Havant, Hayling Island and Fareham and then absorbed societies at Bognor Regis, Petersfield, Winchester, Farnham and Alton.

The Basingstoke Society brought in 18,000 members and an annual trade of £1,400,000. The following year the Andover Society also transferred. After all these mergers, PIMCO had a trading area of over 1,000 square miles, with over a quarter of a million members. By the 1970s the trading area had increased to some 1,600 square miles and around 4,000 staff were employed.

PIMCO introduced some new ideas and some new styles of advertising. And they seemed to be doing well. In May 1969 the Directors announced:

> Despite the huge bill of £400,000 a year for Selective Employment Tax, the increase in Corporation Tax and many other external cost increases, the Board of Directors of the Portsea Island Mutual Co-operative Society Limited are recommending an interim dividend of 1s 4d in the pound on purchases for the half-year ended March 29 1969.

A hair boutique was opened in July and a "Social Expression Department" sold cards etc in October.

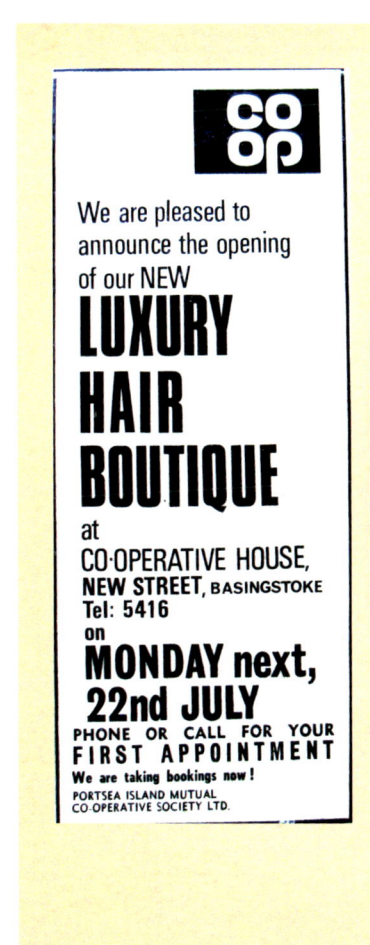

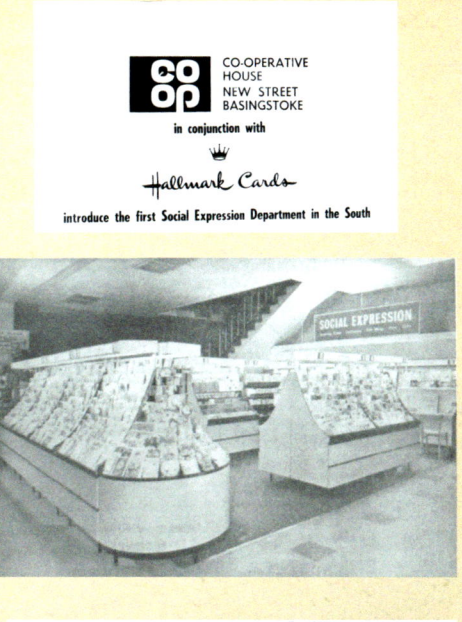

Here you will find, helpfully brought together in a single department, everything you need to express your feelings to your friends. You'll find a dazzling display of greetings cards . . . the very latest in colourful paper tableware for your parties, beautiful gift wrap and ribbons for your presents, wedding stationery, pens, notepaper—everything in fact to keep in touch and show you care. With Christmas and the party season upon us, you'll find everything you need in the Co-op's most exciting department.

THE SEVENTIES

> ... Population 53580 (1971) ... M3 opened (1972) ... Basingstoke District Hospital ...

In 1970 both Marks & Spencers and Woolworths moved into new stores. By 1977 about 400 firms had moved into the town, or set up here, and new industrial and housing estates were built, bringing more customers and the need for more staff.

Staffing

CO-OP VACANCIES
Basingstoke Departmental Store

Deputy Store Manager
Applications are invited from fully experienced men for the position of Deputy to the Store Manager at our Departmental Store 'Co-operative House', New Street, Basingstoke.
Applicants must have wide Departmental Store retail experience and able to act with initiative and to deputise effectively.

Footwear Department
Experienced Senior Saleslady required for Ladies' and Men's Footwear Sections.

Electrical Department
Senior experienced male assistant required for General Electrical Section.

Ladies' Wear and Men's Wear Departments
Senior experienced Sales Lady required for general Ladies' Wear Department and Junior Male Assistant for Men's Wear Department.

Grocery Relief Managers and Grocery Assistants
Experienced male Grocery Staff required for responsible positions as Relief Managers in the Basingstoke area. Average earnings £18/£19 weekly. Vacancies also exist for experienced grocery staff, both male and female.

EXCELLENT WAGES AND CONDITIONS TOGETHER WITH FIVE-DAY, 40 HOUR WEEK AND THREE WEEKS HOLIDAY.

Applications in writing giving details of age, experience etc. to the Personnel Manager, 'Co-operative', 110 Fratton Road, Portsmouth PO1 5DB or by personal call to the local store.

Women too!

CO-OP HAIRDRESSING APPRENTICES

A CAREER IN HAIRDRESSING WITH THE CO-OPERATIVE

If you have decided on hairdressing as a career, then where do you start?
Obviously with an organisation with years of experience in the art of hairdressing and training techniques ... an organisation which has produced many of the top stylists in the area and won over 50 of Britain's coveted trophies and awards ...
After your initial Induction Training a regular period will be set aside each week for theoretical and practical training to give you a thorough understanding of the science of hairdressing.
If you have left school or if you are 15 and wish to join us on leaving school, we will arrange an interview NOW and employ you in school holidays and Saturdays so that you receive initial training.

NO CHARGES OR PREMIUMS

CO-OP DAIRY SALES STAFF
£85+ PER WEEK
BASINGSTOKE

CO-OP BUTCHERY MANAGER – BASINGSTOKE

If you are an experienced Butcher why not join Britain's biggest butcher and get all the benefits, including excellent wages, holidays, staff discount and transferable pension scheme.

These vacancies are open to both male and female applicants.

Savings

January 1970 began with a Super Savers offer (a 16 oz tin of Heinz baked beans, an 8 oz tin of Ovaltine or 1 lb of Kangaroo Australian Butter at 3s). The following year had Summer Specials in the New Street and Sarum Hill stores. There was a terrible pun and a tongue twister in "**Prices hit the floor—Co-op cuts cost of Kosset Carpets!**"

Stamps, like coins, had to go decimal, you could get double stamps on your wig or your freezer and you were encouraged to "become a stamp collector". You could invest in the Co-op too: £5 escalator loans or £50 development bonds. 1972 seemed quieter, with just 10% off made-to-measure suits (super cloths - great patterns).

Was this the first use of the term **Top of the town**?

1973 was a great year! The PIMCO centenary was celebrated with great panache and a double-page advertisement for extra stamps in the *Gazette*.

New ventures

In 1971 the New Street store was brought up to date, with the welcome addition of an off-licence. The same year the *Gazette* reported on the Co-op's plans for a cafeteria, but by April the following year this had been upgraded.

Off-licence for Co-op

AN off-licence for the Basingstoke Co-operative Society's store in New Street, Basingstoke, was provisionally granted by the local Licensing Justices on Tuesday. The Justices were told that structural alterations are to take place in the store.

The butcher's shop will be incorporated inside a new main food hall, with modernisation of the self-service arrangements in the store.

The wines and spirits section will not be self-service. Work will start on the alterations early in the New Year.

Co-op to have cafeteria

AN ironmongers' and tobacconists' premises in Basingstoke's old town centre have now been demolished to make way for two new properties.

The Co-op has demolished Crate's, the tobacconists' old shop in Winchester Street to make way for an extension to their New Street store.

The ground floor of the extension will be a self-service cafataria, and the first floor will be used to extend the main store. The Society also has plans to remodel the present Food Hall. No firm opening date for the extension has been fixed, but it will definitely be open by Christmas.

Opposite the Town Hall, Kingdon's old shop has been demolished to make way for new premises for Hardy's, the Winchester Street furnishing store.

NOW OPEN New Street

The New RESTAURANT ADJOINING Co-operative House Basingstoke

90 Seater Self-Service Restaurant and Steak Bar

OPEN DURING STORE HOURS
9 am to 5.30 daily
6.30 Friday
Early Closing Thursday

Good Food at Popular Prices

PLUS CO-OP STAMPS

MORNING COFFEE
LUNCHES
AFTERNOON TEAS

co op 4 stamps for every 5p spent
PORTSEA ISLAND MUTUAL CO-OPERATIVE SOCIETY LTD

Now there was a laundry and dry cleaning service, a Christmas toy fair and fuel.

co op LAUNDRY AND DRY CLEANING
FOR FAST AND EFFICIENT SERVICE AT DOWN TO EARTH PRICES

LAUNDRY
SHEETS 8p — SHIRTS 7½p
PILLOWCASES 3½p — COAT/OVERALLS 9½p

DRY CLEANING
SUITS AND COATS — Only 40p
TROUSERS AND SKIRTS — Only 20p
DRESSES 32½p — JACKETS 22½p
* FREE RETEXTURING *

Shop service within the week
Weekly van service in most districts
Full details of prices and service from:
SOUTHERN CO-OPERATIVE LAUNDRIES LIMITED
CO-OPERATIVE HOUSE, NEW STREET, BASINGSTOKE
Telephone Basingstoke 4044

Bring the kids to the **co op** Toy Fair

THEY CAN VISIT FATHER CHRISTMAS IN HIS GROTTO AND SEE ONE OF THE BEST SELECTIONS OF TOYS IN TOWN!

New St., Basingstoke
Portsea Island Mutual Co-operative Society Ltd.

TAKE A TIP
Stock up now with Co-op Fuel
You'll not only save £2.00 per ton on the October prices-you'll get
DOUBLE STAMPS
during the month of September

NEW STREET, BASINGSTOKE
Telephone Basingstoke 4044

COME **CO-OP** FOR **SOLID FUEL**

CO-OP SOLID FUEL IS COMPETITIVELY PRICED

CO-OP STAMPS mean that you can save ££s on your heating costs

Order from your local Grocery Branch or from Order Office, NEW STREET, BASINGSTOKE. Telephone 64044
Portsea Island Mutual Co-operative Society Ltd.

There were new promotions in 1979 :

WIN A NIGHT OUT WITH JIMMY SAVILE
and help raise money for charity *

Buy any of these Hoover appliances and you could win a day out in London for two, £50 spending money, **Dinner with Jimmy Savile** and overnight hotel accommodation.

Hoover offers

Automatic washing machine *plus free 20-piece tea set*	£239.95
Junior cleaner	£57.95
Senior cleaner	£59.95

Colour for Christmas
2 Months Free Viewing (on initial payment)
Plus Free Installation
Reliable Service - Stand on castors
Plus Dividend Stamps on all payments
Carefree viewing brought to you by the best in Advanced Technology. Remote control models available - Our rental agreements are backed by our fast reliable team of engineers - No hidden costs - Black & white receivers also available
from **£8·67** monthly
Pay 6 months in advance and view for eight months
RENTACOLOUR
New Street, Basingstoke
co-op

OPENING MONDAY NEXT JULY 26th
The New Self-Service **GROCERY** AT
Winklebury Centre
Basingstoke
Don't MISS the EXTRA OPENING OFFERS IN PRICE CUTS + STAMPS!
CO-OP
PORTSEA ISLAND MUTUAL CO-OPERATIVE SOCIETY LTD.

Winklebury

In 1971 a new self-service Co-op grocery shop opened in the Winklebury Centre, which had just been built off Winklebury Way. This Centre served the growing Winklebury Estate and also housed the Winklebury Estate Office and a newsagents.

Milk deliveries

Milk deliveries had changed too.

Sarum Hill

It had once been a cinema.
   Paul Bosley

> A lovely old building. You used to go in to this great massive place, and then about half way along you'd have the cash office on the right hand side. Mary Kearney used to work in there. And Vera Cubitt, Mary Wason, Alan Andrews and Nobby Clarke. And my boss, John Cooper. One of the best bosses I ever worked for, even today. A lovely bloke, really nice.
>
> You used to have all the furniture all out everywhere. And it still had the stage at the back. And then you could go down in the dungeons where we used to make the tea and that - well, I called them the dungeons. But one day I remember, because it was an old cinema, climbing up at the front of the building and getting into the old projection room. The door was still locked and they still had the old painted boards advertising the films. They still had them up there locked away. And that was the 70s. I actually went in the old projection room.

'Shall we dance?' in old Co-op store plea to planners

A DANCE HALL in the centre of Basingstoke may be a reality after all — if the Co-operative Society go ahead with a new attempt to get planning permission for their furniture store conversion. The planners turned down a recent application by them to turn the store in Sarum Hill into a hall where dances and similar functions could be held.

The large Co-op store which could be converted into a dance hall — but not for two years.

Although the planners had rejected the application for a dance hall, an article in the *Basingstoke Gazette* for 8th December, 1972 reported that the Mayor had asked all the parties involved to look at the matter again. The society's architect, Marcus I Pegg, said it would take up to two years to turn the old store into a dance hall. "We've become increasingly aware that there is a need for a banqueting hall - mainly for private functions like dances and dinners which would probably be held in the evenngs. We feel this building could be successfully converted for that use and it would take about 200 people. There would be kitchen facilities, cloakrooms and so on."

But the following year carpets and furniture were still to be found at Sarum Hill. Paul Bosley started working from there in 1974. By 1975 the old Masonic Hall had been incorporated into the Co-op building, so now there was space for a much wider range of furniture to be displayed.

Apply within.
Paul Bosley

I have fond memories, very fond memories of the Co-op. I saw an advertisement in the window of the Sarum Hill furniture department, saying "Driver's mate wanted. Apply within." So I did. And I got the job, helping the driver, helping hump things round, and making sure he found his way to the right address. We took everything that you could possibly imagine, from a bag of coal or some cushions to a huge great big dining room suite. We delivered everything and anything. It was delivery for New Street as well, Sarum Hill was just the furniture store and around next door was all electrical and everything else and we delivered all that as well.

My driver then was Harry Simmonds, we got on really well. I was there for about five years, To be honest, those were probably the happiest five years that I've ever had working. It was a really nice time. It was always with the same driver, unless he was on holiday. We had some really good laughs, blokes being blokes.

It was a cracking little job. I always remember, in the 1970s there was a woman who was always ordering things; she was an old lady, pretty well confined to the home. And she always made us a cup of tea, the foulest tea that you ever tasted, she put tons and tons of sugar in it. And one day she made us this cup of tea, she stood there talking to us, we didn't want to drink it, me and Harry. And she said, "Do you want a biscuit?" We said, "Yes, please," and with that we tipped our cups of tea on her daffodils. A couple of days later we went back, her daffodils were dead.

The farthest I went in those days, it wouldn't be that far, it would probably be Tadley, Basing, Overton, things like that, towards Reading or down Portsmouth being the furthest, because different branches covered certain areas and we just covered the Basingstoke area.. You had to find your way to some rather strange country lanes. Oh, talk about living and learning, you'd see all these places you'd never even heard of or dreamt of, these little tiny villages. All we had then was a few battered maps, and follow the signposts and that was it really. We did get lost a few times, especially when we was stuck in the snow, it used to snow back then.

Later on we used to do the Andover branch, me and Harry, as well, two days a week, on a Tuesday and Thursday, and we used to go out to tiny little places like Abbots Ann and Little Ann, a beautiful part of the country – well, it was then, it's all built up a lot more these days. But it used to be a good part of the job, going out into the country, especially on nice sunny days. It was a happy five years with Harry, I really enjoyed it.

We had the old Leyland truck, double declutch, OTP703H, I still remember the registration, That was a right old banger, but it went, reliable. And he always drove 30 miles an hour, everywhere. Even when he went to Andover he always drove 30 miles an hour. He wasn't a fast person at all. So it used to take us about an hour to get to Andover, I reckon.

Soper Grove

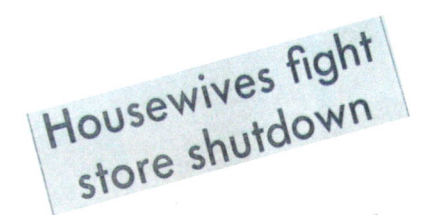

Housewives fight store shutdown

Shoppers siege at closedown store

ANGRY housewives are arming themselves with protest petitions to sabotage the shut down of their "corner store".

The women are shareholders of the Co-operative Wholesale Society at Soper Grove, South View Estate, one of six in the Basingstoke area.

BG 3.10.1975

Mr Tucker, the Co-op spokesman, said that mounting transport costs had jeopardised the delivery service. Basingstoke was the last area in the society's 2,000 square-mile territory (from the Isle of Wight to North Hampshire) to continue home deliveries, and Soper Grove was the last of 125 branches to phase out the service.

But despite the protests, the Soper Grove store was closed and outstanding stock was transferred to other stores in the town.

The Co-op Rooms

After the Co-op moved out . . .
Shelagh le Marechal

In 1974 the Basingstoke Borough Council allowed the Brookvale Community Association (BCA) to use the rooms upstairs in the former Co-op offices in Essex Road. Until then the BCA had met in people's houses, empty shops and at the Technical College but the Co-op rooms were much larger and, because the BCA alone used them, were much more useful.

The BCA had been formed by local residents to run social activities, give support to neighbours and help with local problems, run activity groups and raise money for the village hall.

Ken McSteen, who was chairman of the BCA at that time, and Ruth Buckingham, another founder member, said the rooms were very dirty and they had to clean and scrub everywhere, including the store room which still had its trap-door and winching equipment. Everywhere had to be painted with fire-resistant paint and hung with fire-resistant curtains. Ken said the most remarkable room was the beautifully panelled boardroom, which had an enormous table in it. This table, which seated at least 24, had been made on site so could not be removed when the Co-op left the premises. Otherwise the rooms were empty.

The BCA held committee meetings in the rooms but it was also the venue for Art and Crafts exhibitions, Jumble Sales, a Medieval Banquet and local groups, including a mother and toddler group started by Lynne Manners. There were many children's activities and parties and it was a hive of activity, with lots of fund-raising events.

Basingstoke Direct Mail Service used the downstairs area and eventually the BCA let out some of the area to Basingstoke Boxing Club and then to the Basingstoke Caribbean Association. By 1982-3 the BCA Village Hall was built and they left the Co-op rooms for good. The Co-op rooms had given the BCA the opportunity to have a base for its organisation and its activities.

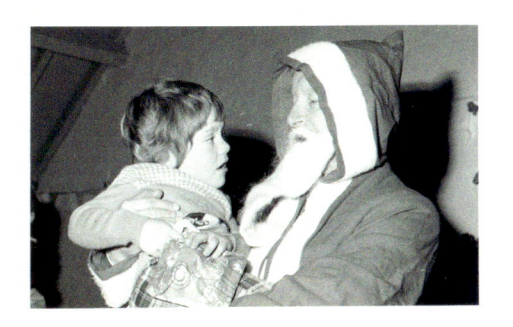

The Co-operative Women's Guild

In July 1970 Mr Young of the County Health Department spoke to the meeting on Drug Addiction, which was on the increase in Basingstoke, with the 15 to 18 years age group particularly at risk in experimenting. There was a proposal that proceeds from the Guild's July Sale should be donated to the Peruvian Earthquake Fund.

The Christmas lunch, prepared by the Social Committee, was followed by the exchange of gifts and a raffle. Prizes were awarded for the best home-made snowman and Christmas tree, followed by carol singing and a variety of games.

The following year the Guild gave a special welcome to eight elderly patients from Basing Road Hospital and three members of the nursing staff who accompanied them. They were entertained by the Vintage Players, who presented two short plays. At their Christmas lunch the National President of the Co-operative Women's Guild told Basingstoke members that they should become involved in the future of education, especially with school meals and milk, and that they should maintain and sustain the democracy of the community.

The Basingstoke CWG had been represented on the Federation of Basingstoke Societies, but in January 1972 it was reported that the affairs of the Federation were about to be terminated

> At the first New Year's meeting of the Co-operative Women's Guild, the chairman (Mrs. T. Oliver) welcomed two new members. Mrs. P. M. Miller reported on a special meeting of the Federation of Basingstoke Societies, at which it was decided that the affairs of the Federation should be terminated at the next annual meeting in February.

It was a time of endings. In 1979 Arthur Attwood had a full-page article in the *Basingstoke Gazette* giving the history of the Basingstoke branch of the Co-operative Women's Guild over the past 80 years, with the message that the Guild was likely to fold unless a new secretary could be found,. We have no record of meetings after that but the Guild did continue in other parts of The Southern Co-operative area. The Centenary was celebrated in 1993.

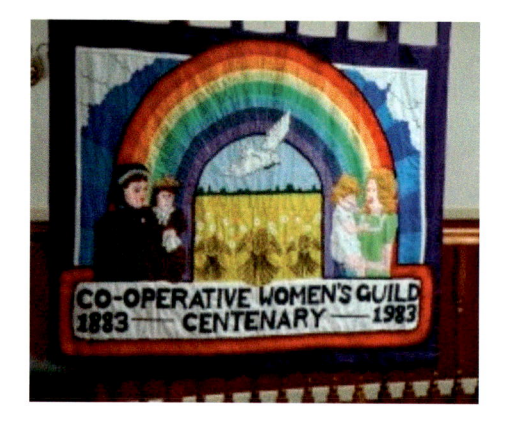

THE EIGHTIES AND NINETIES

... The Malls shopping centre ... Provident Life. ... Sun Life of Canada ...

In the early 1980s advertisements in the *Gazette* seemed rather uninspired, though there were offers of double and treble stamps and even a 'Two for the price of one' offer, oddly enough, on a rental TV. Divans, continental quilts and music centres were bringing the customer up to date.

In 1982 adverts were covering two Co-operative Department Stores - New Street, Basingstoke and High Street, Alton.

115

On 9th September 1983 the Gazette carried the startling headline.

"Scheme to pull down Co-op"

PIMCO now wanted to relocate in Basingstoke "because the New Street site is no longer appropriate since the town's new shopping centre opened". There had already been redundancies at the store and plans for an out-of-town furniture retail store had been turned down. A spokesman said they were considering a revised application for a furniture retail store "and any further developments would depend on the outcome of future negotiations and planning applications."

In August the *Gazette* carried an article by Arthur Attwood reporting that "The face of Basingstoke continues to change. With the closure of the Co-op food shop at New Street, the top of the town has lost the last of its major grocery shops. At one time this was the main area where housewives re-stocked their larders, week by week." He described the various grocery shops and the growth of the Co-op in the town, pointing out that the Co-op had their own farm to the north of Park Prewett Hospital and their own printing works on the outskirts of Reading. He said, "Today it is the new town centre where the shoppers flock, with Sainsbury's and Tesco's supplying by far the bulk of groceries - not only for Basingstoke but also for a very wide area of north Hampshire. But will the pattern change with the growing practice of supermarkets opening on the estates, as Sainsbury's have done at Brighton Hill? The Co-op tried to do just that but were overtaken by Big Brother."

The following January issues of the *Gazette* carried Co-op advertisements for sales, and in February for Stocktaking Clearance, making way for the next "new shopping experience".

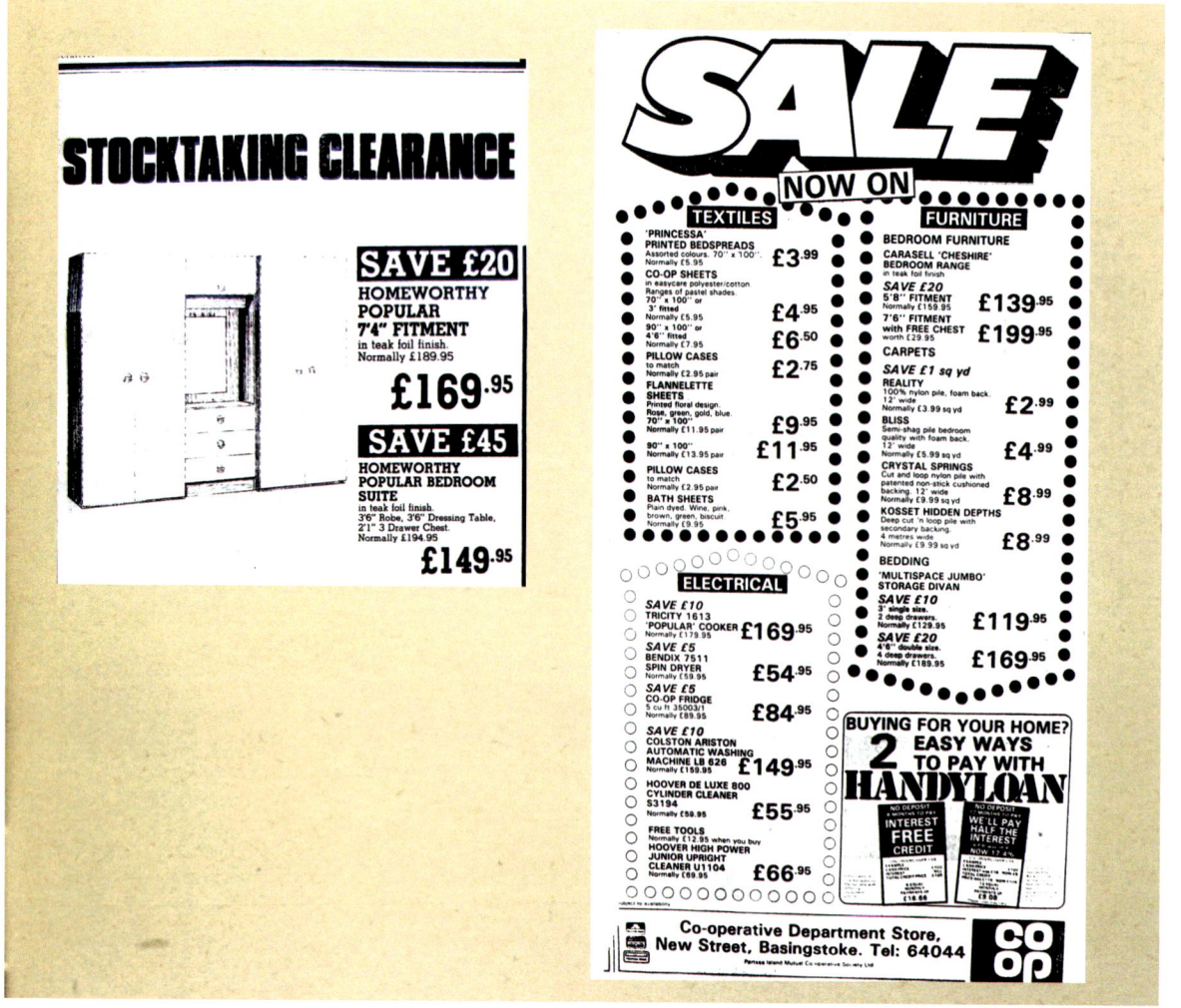

VISTA

Co-op moves into town centre

BG24.2.1984

Demands for another food store in Basingstoke's shopping centre will soon be answered.

Portsea Island Co-op has confirmed it is to move into Tesco's old shop near the public library.

More than 60 new jobs will be created and recruitment has already started.

It is hoped that the store will be ready for business by the middle of next month.

The shop will be the 18th in the Co-op's chain of successful Vista supermarkets, which were first launched three years ago.

It is the society's boast that the stores have a reputation for providing the "highest quality and standards at the lowest prices".

The move to the shopping centre follows the closure, early last year, of the Co-op's food hall at its larger premises in New Street.

A society spokesman said: "The new store will enable us to re-establish ourselves as a major retailing force in the town centre."

The Co-op's decision will be welcomed by many shoppers, especially the elderly.

They were upset at Tesco's move to a modern out-of-town store at Chineham last year.

This has left Sainsbury's with the only supermarket in the shopping precinct.

A Co-op driver

I got pulled out of the snow.
   Paul Bosley

> When I left the Co-op I went to United Linen, I was only there for about six months, and one day I saw our old transport manager, Ron Williams, at Roentgen Road – that's where the transport depot was back then. And he said that they had a new round being created and they wanted a driver. So in 1982 I was back at the Co-op again. And then what I had to do was basically drive down to Fratton Road in Portsmouth, fill up the van and go and deliver, say, restock Farnham store or Petersfield store, or things like that. Gosport, all round there. I had a Leyland Terrier, and I got pulled out of the snow by a tractor down Bramley once.

Things changed.
   Paul Bosley

> Then the Co-op closed down and they opened up in Winklebury as Homemaker in 1984. I was still driving, and I had a brand new Mercedes, very comfy, especially after riding round in that old Leyland Terrier. It was a Luton van with a box section, to deliver all the furniture in.
>
> Homemaker was a big square building, about the size of a football pitch or slightly shorter. Once we went there in 1984 things changed. The people from New Street went up there - we had a few new faces but it was basically the same people.
>
> The management was a lot stricter. It wasn't as good as in the early Co-op days. That's when the Co-op went up from doing the simple cheaper things, tried to move up market, it never worked, and the place was starting to decline. I was there for about three or four years but the money wasn't really good, and then we started a family so I had to find a job with more money, so I left in 1985 and Homemaker closed in 1988.

The Co-operative Women's Guild

Although the Basingstoke Branch of the Co-operative Women's Guild had closed, members from other branches attended a centenary congress in 1992. This was ten years later than the centenary of the Guild - perhaps 100 years after the first congress.

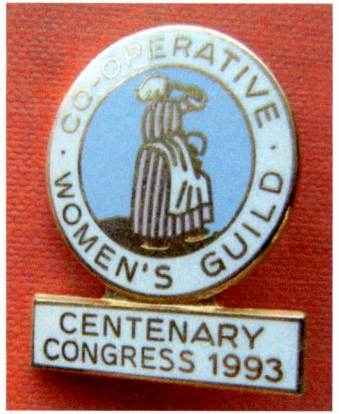

Tadley

The Tadley Branch continued to thrive and to contribute to local affairs.

PIMCO

The 1980s showed a change of emphasis in PIMCO's Member Relations strategy. They introduced the Community Dividend and new forms of member benefits, replacing individual dividend payments and allowing more innovative community activities by the Society.

On its 125th anniversary in 1997 PIMCO changed its name to "Southern Co-operatives Limited" to show that it was now a family of co-operative enterprises, covering much of the South of England. In view of the environmental and social costs of large out-of-town superstores, it was decided to focus on providing a range of services at community level, expanding back into localities from which they had previously withdrawn.

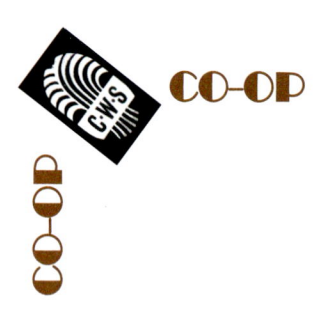

INTO THE 21ST CENTURY

> ... Festival Place shopping centre ...   HQ for Shire Pharmaceuticals and Huawei ...

The Town Centre VISTA found it hard to compete with out of town shopping centres and gave way to various "convenience stores" around the town, in addition to those on outlying estates.

South Ham

From the top to the bottom down...
   Jan Sim

I'm currently the manager at the King's Road Co-op in South Ham. I've been doing this job for around two to three months now and before that I was the deputy manager here for nearly three years. Prior to that I worked for big supermarkets, mostly Morrisons, and that was for about 20 years

The reason I decided to move from a larger supermarket to somewhere like the Co-op was because I'd spent so long there and probably all in all 20 years working for a big player, I decided I needed to try what it was like to work for a different company. I think the thing that attracted me with the Co-op, was that I wouldn't just be doing one department, I'd be doing a lot of other things. You need to know the job really from the top to the bottom down, and that just opened up a lot more areas for me to learn. I think that was basically the reason I did it.

In the bigger supermarkets you tend to specialise in one area. Before I left I was the fresh food manager, so you know fresh foods inside and out. But with the Co-op, as a manager, you need to know everything, from Human Resources to your chill department, from doing wages to booking holidays - just basically everything you have to know. I think the biggest difference I probably noticed when I first came to the Co-op, was that there was a lot more mental work and a lot less physical work. Being a manager on a department at Morrisons, in a really big store, probably meant about 75% of it was physically hard work and the rest was paper work. With the Co-op it's probably the other way around. There's a lot more paper work to do.

The Co-op and the school . . .
Jo Kelly

> The King's Road Co-op in South Ham have, in the past, been giving small prizes for the school where I'm a Governor, because it is their local school, and they will give a prize if the school's having a raffle. At Easter they gave Easter egg prizes for the children who were making Easter gardens. And the year before they did Easter bonnets, and again they had Easter egg prizes.

Buckskin

From the Spar to the Co-op . . .
Sam Austin

> I was born in Basingstoke and worked in the Spar shop in Buckskin. About ten years ago it was taken over by the Co-op and I found that they had quite a different way of working from Spar. It was more structured, with more rules, particularly involving security and I think that was all for the good.
>
> I became the Manager of this shop six years ago. Every Co-op shop is different, depending on the area it is in. Most of our customers are local and regular, as most of them are members of the Co-op, receiving a share in profits. Our shop is next to the Buckskin Community Centre, and we like to get involved with events there. We often give donations, such as vouchers for a raffle, and recently we set up a Fair Trade stand in the Centre.
>
> We don't have any choice of what to sell in the shop, but if a customer asks for something we don't stock we can put it to Head Office and they will try to get it for us. There aren't any changes I would like to make in the shop. I think it works very well as it is.

Overton

I jumped at the opportunity.
Bernard Steele

> I'm from South Africa and my wife and I emigrated to the UK. I had worked in the wholesale trade, supplying supermarkets, and I was looking to get into the same field. When I was doing some shopping in a Southern Co-operative Store in Emsworth it had just been re-fitted and looked fantastic. They had a Community event going on. I thought, "Well, it looks much more fun being on that side of the retail trade, and being able to interact with customers face to face rather than telephonically." The store was vibrant, everybody having a good time. So I went home and read up about The Southern Co-operative and I applied for a job there the same day. It wasn't long before I was sent on the Manager's course. Then I was asked to come and run the Overton Branch and I jumped at the opportunity.
>
> I was met by my deputy, Barbara, and she was the best tour guide I'd ever met. I think within half an hour I got the whole tour and history of Overton and the Basingstoke area, it was brilliant. What appealed to me immediately about the village was the way everybody knew everybody and everybody looked out for one other.

When you combine that with the Co-operative principles it really is a match made in heaven for anybody who likes that kind of environment.

In the Overton store we are tied closely with the local community. During Christmas the local Scouts group came and did some bag packing to raise some much needed funding for a Jamboree they are attending. We also had various fund-raising initiatives, a tea and cake morning and a dress-up day, all in aid of our corporate charity of the year, C.H.I.C.K.S. We frequently host the Hampshire Wildlife Trust in our store to get their message out and we try and do that with all our partners. We sponsor a lot of local charities or local events, for example the Overton Primary School and food and raffle prizes for St Mary's Church summer camp. To be seen to make a positive contribution to the community and be part of that, to make a difference, is a privilege. The Southern Co-operative actively encourages us to do that. We're not a big, bad corporate. Our contribution to the community is really at the heart of everything we do.

Every four years there is a Sheep Fair in Overton and it is the next event we are preparing for. We will be supporting it as much as we can. It will be my first time so I'm looking forward to getting involved. We will probably have a raffle, a dress-up day and have a stall.

In my time we sponsored various people, charities and events. One that stands out is sponsoring a few of the Fire fighters doing the Ben Nevis Challenge. I think they're probably in the right sort of profession to do that. If I were to try it I don't think I'd make it. It involves climbing Ben Nevis, Scafell and Mount Snowdon, driving between them, all within twenty-four hours. So that is twenty miles of walking, with ten thousand feet of climbing, plus five hundred miles of driving, which is not a feat to be sneezed at. We were very happy to be able to provide them with food. It was a success for them.

We also assisted the 1st Overton Scout Group. They have a yearly summer camp, for kids between the ages of ten and fourteen; there is quite a cost to the Scout Group to hold these events and we arranged some vouchers for them and helped to raise some money to hold the camp,

The highlight of the year has been launching our Community Support Card. We took nominations from local organisations and charities and we aim to raise £10,000 to be split between the Kingfisher Day Centre and the Overton School Association. Customers are given a Community Support Card which we will swipe at every transaction they make and a portion of the sale goes to the fund, at no cost to the customer! It's a fantastic way to give something back. We launched it with a fun day: we had a bouncy castle, a barbecue, arts and crafts, tea and cake, a bird show, zumba dancing and an Easter egg hunt. We tried to involve as many local traders as we could. It was a fantastic success and it was very well supported by the people of Overton.

Bernard receiving an award from the Basingstoke & Deane Borough Council, March 2011

Beggarwood Lane

Onwards and Upwards!
Peter Cole

I was born in Peckham, South London. After school I had various jobs in retail but my main career was working in outsize men's clothing. I've worked for the Co-op for ten years. At that time I could see that The Southern Co-op was growing its business in Basingstoke and there would be opportunities here. I have moved around the various stores quite a lot. I first started work in the Buckskin store and then moved to South Ham and later to Tadley.

I opened the Beggarwood store six years ago. At that time the worry was there were not many houses round it. But of course people thinking of buying one of the new houses being built were delighted to find our store within easy reach.

Three years ago I went to Odiham when The Southern Co-operative were introducing their new concept - you might think that was basically new flooring and things like that, but really it was concentrating on local farm produce. Then I went to Aldershot and then back to Beggarwood. I love it there!

There are differences between the various stores, reflecting the tastes of people in each area. For instance, speaking generally, in South Ham cigarettes and beer are in demand and you must never run out. At Beggarwood we have grown our fresh foods, local sausages, fresh vegetables, salads and we have a big in-house bakery, making fresh bread and croissants. We don't sell a great deal of beer. Alcohol sales are mainly wine and lager.

Almost opposite the Co-op is a day nursery. We give them vouchers which we get from head office; we have a budget for them each year. This last year and the year before we provided vouchers for the Naomi House Jack's Place, and this year we will all be taking part in the RadCan Walk (a new charity which has been set up to provide a radiotherapy facility at the Basingstoke & North Hants Foundation Trust Hospital).

We have been growing year on year very well, and we hope to continue onwards and upwards.

Odiham

Hen and duck eggs . . .
Dan Rapson

I come from a family that has been in the retail business in north Hampshire for many years, so I learnt about small stores as a child. Whilst I was still at school I had a part-time job at a Sainsbury store. At seventeen I joined them full time and became a trainee manager. I was lucky; at that time they ran a scheme where they assisted you with a grant whilst you studied at university to gain retail management qualifications. You had to agree to work for the company for five years after you received them. It was a good scheme. Unfortunately they no longer run such a system. A shame. After nine and a half years I went to Boots for two years, so I had eleven and a half years in retail before I joined the Co-op.

I came to work with the Co-op just over a year ago. The first four months I undertook the initial training which involved working in various stores within the Southern Co-operative group and attending training courses.

I came to this store in April 2011 as the Retail Business Manager. This post is the manager of a community store, which Odiham is. You have the task of running the store as if it is a stand-alone store in the local community. I enjoy this challenge. The emphasis here is on local produce, which I source from the area. The biggest sellers in the store at the moment are the local hen and duck eggs. We also sell local cakes, pastries, biscuits, jams, pickles, sausages - the list goes on expanding. I think this is an important part of being a community store.

Another part is becoming involved with the local area and its groups and charities. At Christmas we helped various groups and schools, we gave out six hampers and six vouchers. We have one particular local charity that we are closely involved with. A colleague, Jack Bland, was killed in a "hit and run" accident, he was only nineteen years old, so we are involved with the "Jack Bland Memorial Fund". This year we took part in Odiham's Macmillan Coffee Morning, for which we provided the milk, tea, coffee, biscuits and of course some cakes. Then there is the local Blues and Booze Festival. That is great fun; the main organisers are RAF Odiham. There is always some local event we are part of. That helps make the job.

The future? I would like to expand the range of local produce but the store is tight for space so we need to enlarge. One thing is certain, though, we are here to stay. Me? My future? I see it with the Southern Co-operative.

Training

...there are teams...
Peter Cole

> The structure in a reasonable sized store is that there are teams; you become a team leader, a deputy manager and then manager. From the start you have to do day training and learning about the Co-op - someone will come and talk to the staff for about an hour.
>
> As soon as you are a team leader you have to do the APLH training, that's a national qualification so that you can be the licence holder in charge of the liquor. You have to do Health and Safety, First Aid and Food and Hygiene training.

...a good way of comparing notes...
Sam Austin

> To become a store manager I did a 6-7 months training period in Portsmouth. This involved courses on personnel, costing procedures, budget costing, estimated turnover and things like that. There was an exam and someone from Human Resources came in to go through the folder that I had to keep records of sales etc. Training is still ongoing, so that managers can be updated about new stock and new procedures and it is a good way of meeting other managers and comparing notes.

...you are not a number...
Dan Rapson

> I have found the Co-op training differs from other retail training courses. There is an emphasis on the ethics and history of the Co-operative Movement. An expectation that whilst it is a modern commercial business you must not forget its origins and ethical foundation. When you work for the Co-op you are not a number, you are an individual. This is what I like.

Winklebury Way

We're going to Ghana.
Jako Carstens

> Fort Hill Community School has developed a relationship with the Winklebury store run by The Co-operative Group. It all started when our students made Fairtrade buntings and posters. I contacted the Co-op manager (Jon Grouse) and he agreed to put the posters & buntings up as a display, along with some Fairtrade items they sell in the shop.
>
> We asked the *Gazette* to take a photo of the display, with some of our students. While we were waiting for the photographer, I told Jon about our link school in Ghana. He was very interested and keen to get involved. I came up with the following project idea.

Mr Wright and I went on a teacher visit to Ghana in April 2011. and during the visit a class of students walked to the local grocer to pick out items that would also be found in the Co-operative in Winklebury. The basket, containing 13 items, was taken back to the school, where students had to estimate the total and the cost in the UK. We also looked at food miles, Olympic menus, exchange rates and cost of living.

When two of their teachers came on a reciprocal visit in July 2011, we did the same with a group of our students. The basket of items was taken to school for all students to do the activity. Our feeder primary schools also made visits to the Co-op for the same project.

Invoice: Ghana **7 April 2011**		Invoice: Winklebury **10 June 2011**	£
Sultana Spaghetti	1.20		
Weetabix (24)	8.50	Weetabix	1.99
Full cream boxed milk (even 1 litre)	5.50	CP Unit milk	0.84
Coke can	1.20	Coca Cola	0.65
Beans (Heinz tin)	3.00	Hz baked beans	0.64
Tomato ketchup (Heinz small)	3.50	Tomato ketchup	1.24
Marmalade (from Holland)	5.00	Orange marmalade	1.29
Toothpaste (Close Up)	2.00	Colgate Reg Toothpaste	1.45
Tetley teabags (40)	5.50	Teabags	1.26
Shortbread (McVities 100g)	3.50	CP S/bread Fingers	1.19
Bar of soap (Jergens)	1.20	Dove cleansing bar	0.65
Cream Crackers (Jacobs 200g)	2.00	Jacobs Cream Crackers	0.89
Sugar bread loaf	1.50	1 Warbs Farmhouse	1.42
TOTAL Cedis	**43.80**		
(43 Ghanaian Cedis, 80 Pesewas = **£18.25**)			
TOTAL	**£18.25**	**TOTAL**	**£13.51**

CAR WASH AT THE CO-OP STORE!

SAT 24TH MARCH
From 11am
£5 a CAR!

ALL MONEY GOES TOWARDS FORT HILL COMMUNITY SCHOOLS GHANA PROJECT!

6 students from Fort Hill Community school are going Akropong in Ghana to meet their link school. All money raised is going towards buying sports equipment and a litter clean-up campaign.

Tadley

Making a difference . . .
Michelle Stoessel

I have been an employee of the Co-op for less than a year. I previously worked as an area manager in the fuel industry so it is a real change of direction for me to become manager of the Tadley Co-op. I made a conscious decision to find a company that believes in being involved with and working with its local community. It is a thing that I strongly believe in. I have three children and I want them to understand the worth of working with and for society. Making a difference.

Tadley is a local community store. We aim to stock a range of local produce - for example, locally baked cakes, jam and biscuits. We also have local beers and cider.

Last Christmas we helped local charities and organisations with donations and vouchers. We provided 130 mince pies for one group. Another was having a Fair Trade event so we gave a range of our Fair Trade goods.

The Co-operative ideals

Why I joined the Co-operative Party . . .
David Carr

I always had an interest in mutuality and the Co-operative ideal, and in 2003 Alan Evans and Mike Tiller gave a presentation on what the Co-op Party was about. So I decided to join the Co-operative Party and I have attended regularly ever since. Discussions take place on how co-operation can apply to situations, especially where there is a service missing, and how to get people involved to bring these ideals about as the Rochdale Pioneers did.

Co-op funerals

In 1956 the Furnishing Department in Winchester Street undertook funerals, as had many furnishing shops before then.

In 2010 The Co-operative funeral care came to Basingstoke

**BASINGSTOKE CO-OPERATIVE SOCIETY LTD.
UNDERTAKERS**
Complete Funeral Furnishers
Cremations   Moderate Charges
Furnishing Department:
WINCHESTER ST., BASINGSTOKE
Phone Basingstoke 854/5

...of some service...
Criss Connor

Now that I have retired I have become a reserve funeral assistant for The Southern Co-operative. Having been involved in voluntary organisations, I felt that this was some other way of being able to serve people. Here they are in a state of mourning and they want someone to look after their departed, and I thought I could just be of some service to them in that respect.

...a very testing and sensitive line of work...
Gavin Denman

I have been in the funeral profession for a number of years now, starting as a Driver/Bearer and Funeral Operative (Assistant), and then progressing through to arranging and conducting the funerals as a Funeral Director. I am now managing six branches and, although this can be a very testing and sensitive line of work, it is also an extremely rewarding one. There is nothing more satisfying than being able to help a family through the most difficult time of their lives.

The Southern Co-operative Funeralcare now has 17 funeral homes in Hampshire, with others covering Berkshire, Surrey, Sussex and recently three new premises on the Isle of Wight. The Basingstoke branch in Buckland Avenue was opened in 2010.

The funeral profession has changed over the last thirty years to accommodate changes that have happened in society, communities and families, and the choices available increase every day. So the family's expectations of a good funeral service have changed too.

We feel that attention to detail is absolutely critical at all times. Each colleague has undergone extensive and comprehensive training in every aspect of the profession: driving a limousine, bearing at a funeral, arranging the funeral service or conducting the funeral on the day. The

Southern Cooperative's training programmes are second to none. They include one-to-one mentoring, electronic 'E-learning', attendance at courses and seminars and more formally recognised NVQ and Diploma courses offered by The National Association of Funeral Directors (NAFD).

The process of arranging a funeral can obviously be a very difficult and worrying time for the family who are left behind. We are aware of this and ensure that we take as much of the burden away from the family as we possibly can. We guide our families in choosing from the variety of options available and we help them build a meaningful, unique service. Once the decisions are made, we will make all the necessary telephone calls and set up meetings for the family with their chosen officiate, who will look after the actual funeral service for them. Every aspect is looked after with the utmost care and attention to detail by the dedicated team. We offer the same care as we would to one of our own family.

There can be different modes of transport, including the standard Motor Hearse, a Motorcycle Hearse, a Horse Drawn Carriage or a Land Rover 4X4 Hearse. There are different styles of coffins, with wicker and bamboo being very popular, along with painted and decorated picture coffins, and there is an array of various containers for cremated remains. Methods of disposal include not only burial or scattering of ashes but also turning into gemstones and even being included in a firework display.

During the time of organising the funeral and the weeks and months following, we are able to offer our families the support of our Bereavement Centre, run by Ingrid McAllister-Derry, who is a volunteer for Cruse Bereavement Care, a qualified Counsellor and a Professional Life Coach.

The Bereavement Centre is able to offer one-to-one counselling, support and friendship groups to the bereaved, as well as providing education to other professionals in the form of Bereavement Workshops and Study Days. It is a completely free-of-charge service and is available to any families who need our support, whether they have used our services or not.

Pre-paid Funeral Plans are becoming increasingly popular as more people want to make sure their wishes are known to their families and to remove the financial burden from them. The Co-operative Funeral Bond offers peace of mind to all concerned, knowing that everything is in place and paid for. It is fully guaranteed and therefore inflation proof. All aspects of the funeral can be covered, including transport, flowers, service cards and charitable donations, along with the fees paid to third parties (disbursements) which include churches, ministers, crematoria and medical fees. Every Bond is bespoke to the client's wishes.

In my Will...
Jo Kelly

I've already left a little note with my Will that I want a Co-op funeral, and I do hope that somebody who's a member actually pays the bill so that they get the points on my funeral.

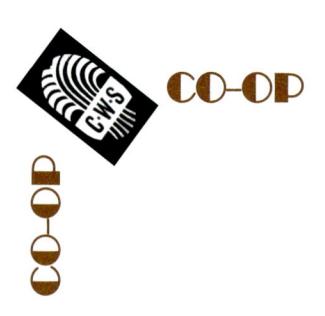

LOOKING BACK AND LOOKING FORWARD

... Basingstoke memories and archives / Websites / What will come next ? ...

In a Museum

An early 20th century PIMCO store has been recreated in "Milestones" - Hampshire's Living History Museum in Basingstoke. To set this up The Southern Co-operative worked in partnership with experts from Hampshire Museums Service. The store has a typical PIMCO frontage with goods of the time displayed in the windows. The displays are changed from time to time to reflect different events, such as Queen Victoria's Jubilee, or Christmas.

When you go inside there are illustrated booklets on lecterns, giving background information and there is a video explaining the Co-operative ethos.

Even more dramatic is the realistic mannequin of the provision hand behind the counter, ready to serve you.

Sponsored by the Co-op, Milestones volunteers have helped Museum Service staff to restore a Co-op milk lorry. They built the cab and body and used the chassis from a derelict vehicle.

The Southern Co-operative

In 2009 the name was changed once again, to a more succinct version.

The Southern Co-operative

A fun environment. . . .
Bernard Steele

We are an independent Co-operative, called The Southern Co-operative. We are based mostly in the South of England and we are fiercely independent although we are adopting the national brand. We remain entrenched in our original communities down south, which puts us in a prime position to really be part of those communities. We've had a long history with the people in and around the villages and towns where we operate. As a Co-operative we want to be seen as your local store, as a meeting place in the community where people come and say 'Hi!', not just to do their shopping. I see it every day in my store where people come in, they are chatting in the aisle and they're catching up, and that's great and that's what it is. We're like a central hub. And we put a lot of emphasis on getting to know the community and assisting the community where we can. That was one of the reasons why I applied for the job at the Co-op. Their sense of ethics, with fair trade, the fact that everybody's a member and everybody has a say in the running of the Co-operative . One can go on to the website and find many instances, photos and videos of the good work we're doing in the communities.

I think with the national brand we're all adopting a single face to the public and it'll clear up a little bit of confusion. For The Southern Co-operative it'll just see us entrenching ourselves more within the communities. When I think of village life in England I think of your butcher, your baker, and the Co-operative will be as much a part of the village as those trades, while actively supporting them. We're not here to replace anybody, we are here to add value. And it'll all really be about creating a focus on community, serving our customers, putting their needs first, so we're always open to ideas and we're nimble enough to adapt with the times and move where our customers need us to go.

We're not too big. We've had about a hundred and fifty stores, I think at this stage, and it's a manageable size and it allows us to react quickly to the market, especially now that the economy in the financial situation is on everybody's thoughts at the moment. We see ourselves putting the customer first, listening to what our customers have to say and, hopefully, through meetings and customer focus groups we'll be able to steer our business in a direction that's suitable for the village or town and the people in it.

For anybody working in the Co-op it's really an exciting environment. It's kind of the best of both worlds because every day's a challenge, every day you are coming in doing a hard day's work but getting to meet people and talk to people, you're not necessarily stuck in an office the whole day and it's just a great way to get involved in the community and just a fun environment.

In our store we're like a little team. I think that store levels are a microcosm of the whole Co-operative. We get together and we're always helping; stores will often e-mail to say they need some help in this area or that and we all pitch in where we can. I think it's in the name, the Co-operative, we do actively try and co-operate with each other and that's the way forward.

So that everyone benefits . . .
Ted Merdler

The Southern Co-operative of today is in some ways very different from the old Basingstoke Co-operative, but in others, surprisingly similar. Many of the products we sell today would be unrecognisable to the founders of the Basingstoke Co-op: would they have ever have dreamt of "smoothies" or "microwaveable" food? They would, of course, recognise just about all of the fresh food items although we suspect that today's storage systems keep them a lot fresher!

Although we are a business with a multi-million pound turnover, employing nearly 3,500 people, trading across the south of England, we still believe in and actively follow the values and principles that the original co-operators would have known. Each member is entitled to one vote and we work with other co-operatives and member-owned organisations so that everyone benefits. Shopper members still get a "dividend" or, as it is called nowadays, "a share of the profits". We still firmly believe that to be a successful business we must engage with the communities in which we trade and support them in a variety of ways, not only with financial support but also with volunteering and taking part in local events. This involvement means that we can be a truly local business wherever we trade; after all, many of our colleagues will live in the town or village, their children will go to the local school and they will be involved in many local activities - they are themselves "local" and already part of their community.

In addition to our food stores, we also have Funeral Homes. Once again they are part of the community, helping at local events and supporting local people through troubled times when they have experienced a bereavement.

The Southern Co-operative also forms relationships with other groups and becomes a "partner". One of our partners is the Hampshire and IOW Wildlife Trust. We work with the Trust to help support important environmental sites in north Hampshire and cattle that graze on those sites have been used to supply top quality beef to stores in the Basingstoke and north Hampshire area only - a truly local initiative which gives environmental benefits in many ways. Indeed, we believe that we need to support local food producers in general, and several of our stores in the area sell locally produced food. This helps to cut down on "food miles", supports a local business and gives our customers the opportunity to buy unique, quality products.

A member's viewpoint

Fish and chips for everybody!
Jo Kelly

Everyone talks about how people used to get their Divi one or twice a year but it wasn't until three years ago that someone asked if I was a Co-op member - I was, because I'd taken over my mother's membership. Then he said, "Oh, you should come once a quarter to Milestones, and you'll get a free biscuit and a cup of coffee, and you get a £5 voucher!" So I went and they gave you a little pep talk about how well The Southern Co-operative were doing, you had your cup of coffee and couple of very nice biscuits, and you were given a £5 voucher to spend in the Co-op .

The Southern Co-operative have now re-launched themselves, and they've gone in with the National Co-op, to run a points system, and if you're a member you have a Co-op card. When you buy any shopping you get your points and once a year it is worked out on the profits that the Co-op have made, and you are given an amount of money. So no longer do you get your £5 voucher, but you do get money once a year, after they have had their Members' Annual Meeting, and the profits have been decided.

The meetings are quite interesting and there are also little outings. At Easter 2011 they had a trip to the Brewery in the Meon Valley, where they had a guided tour and we were able to have as much beer as we wanted, but the Co-op didn't want people drinking on an empty stomach, so they bought in fish and chips for everybody. In the summer it was the Hills Apple Juice orchards and that was a very jolly evening! We again had a tour of the factory and a walk through the different apple orchards, and we were told their history. They also have a Nature Reserve so we heard about the different owls they have there and the different wild life. Then we had an apple-tasting of eleven different types of apple juice and we went home clutching a bottle of apple juice, free from the Co-op.

There are several people from Basingstoke that I've known most of my life and we meet up once a quarter at the Co-op 'do's'. Once it was in Southampton, in a big hotel down on the waterfront. We had the AGM in the morning, a very nice four-course meal at lunchtime, and then we all piled onto a steamer and were taken up both rivers, and given a cream tea. I was amazed because we'd just had this four-course meal and we'd only been sailing for about half an hour, when they said over the tannoy that cream teas were being served and I couldn't believe it because the older people all tore down to get their cream teas! The couple near me said, "Oh, aren't you going for your cream tea?" And I said, "No, I'm still very full!" They said, "Oh, come and get it, then we can take it home with us." So I went and collected my cup of coffee, and they packed away my two scones, my little thing of clotted cream and my little jar of jam. And they were going to have it the next day.

They had a bee-keepers' two-day course, down at Bishop's Waltham, which usually costs £100, and you are able to go on it for £25, so that's very interesting.

They make a big point of being an "ethical retailer". So they're very particular about trying to get local produce to sell. Each store, even the little ones in Basingstoke, are able to give small grants or small prizes.

Each year all the shops in The Southern Co-operative choose a local charity for which they collect money. In 2011 it was Naomi House, and the local shops were doing all sorts of things, taking part in cycle rides and sponsored walks, being put in stocks and having wet sponges thrown at them. They raised £180,000, the shops themselves and their customers. The Southern Co-operative matched it, so that made quite a reasonable amount of money, and in fact it was rounded up to £400,000. This year the big charity is C.H.I.C.K.S., a holiday home for under-privileged children and disadvantaged children living in London and other places in our area.

Someone has just asked me how you become a Co-op member. You can fill in a form in the shop or you contact them on the website, The Southern Co-op, or you can ring the Head Office, which is down in Fareham. You buy a share in the Co-op and the least you can put in is a pound. What they usually do is sign you up, and you don't pay a pound then, but you can use your Co-op card throughout the country, so whichever part of the country you're in, if you go into a Co-op, you produce your card and they put it through the till and you get your points. And at the end of that year, they hold back a pound from whatever money you've got due. So that's how you do it at the moment.

Thoughts for the future

The subtitle of this book is "A story of change". The way the town and the Co-op changed over the years was sometimes in step as one influenced the other, or both reacted to the same external influences, but sometimes one expanded while the other did not.

As a market town, Basingstoke set up its own Co-operative Society and had branches in some of the surrounding villages like Overton and Kingsclere. Perhaps it is significant that Essex Road, where the Co-op first began to grow, was in Newtown, the area into which the town first expanded, mainly to house railway employees in the 1870s. As the economic focus of the town gradually shifted from agriculture to industry, the ethos of co-operation became attractive to the growing working population. The Co-op began to expand along New Street, nearer to the centre of the town, and opened its Furnishing Store in Sarum Hill.

With further town growth into areas like South View and South Ham, the Basingstoke Co-operative Society saw the need to have local stores away from the centre of the town. But it was the imminent influx of new shoppers in the great "London overspill" redevelopment of the 1960s that prompted the opening of Co-operative House, the "wonderful promenade store" that then offered competition with the major shops and Lanham's departmental store.

As many new estates were built around the town, Winklebury and Oakridge acquired Co-op caravans and then shops. Then, as development continued, stiffer competition came from other departmental stores and supermarkets, while shopping habits changed, with movement to out-of-town sites. The Basingstoke Co-operative Society became part of PIMCO. It replaced Co-operative House with the grocery store, VISTA, in the new town centre and moved the furnishing department to Homemaker at Winklebury, but neither was successful for long. At this point it seemed that the town was flourishing but the Co-op was retreating.

However, now the estates - not quite suburbs and not quite villages - are acquiring their own local identity. In its new "convenience stores" the Co-op is building on this sense of locality and community and the sense of ownership by its members.

So what of the future? Basingstoke's economic base is turning more from industry to technology and services. How will this affect the Co-op and what effect will the Co-op continue to have on the town? What changes have we yet to see?

INDEX

Names in **bold** are of people who have been interviewed or told us of their experiences in other ways. Master cassettes, CDs and transcriptions of interviews are held at the Wessex Film & Sound Archive, with copies held by BAHS and the Willis Museum, Basingstoke. Accession numbers are given in brackets in three sequences. M = Willis Museum recordings; BAHS = BAHS recordings on cassette; BTH = BAHS digital recordings.

A

advertising policy 2,3,16,63-4
Alton 49,104,115
Andrews, Alan (BTH 057) 2,72,84,95-6,110
Andrews, Mary 84
Applin, Bob (BAHS 001) 75
Architects: Wallis & Smith 7,23,39; Ekins, L G 41,43,44; Wallis, Richard Sterry 11,14
Assembly Hall 15,16; Assembly Rooms 11
Attwood, Arthur (M 010) 42,116
Austin, Sam 121,125
AWRE 69

B

bakery 8,11,12, 21,24,30,40-2,48,51,62,70,71,74,82, 84,85,91,123
bands
  Basingstoke North Hants Band 53; Borough Band 35; Brass Band from Methodist Church 55; Brian Thornton's Silver Prize Accordion Band 53; Mechanics' Institute Band 27; North Hants Iron Works Band 26,47; Sarum Hill Methodist Band 53; Stan Rogers and his Blue Star Players 83; String band 16
Basingstoke
  changes in shopping patterns 1,3,5,85,116,117, 133;   economic focus 35;   population 5,7,11,15,39,50,53,69,85,88,106,135;   redevelopment 1,5,85-6,88
Basingstoke Carnival 56
Basingstoke Borough Council 48,49, 50,60,85,113; & Deane 122
Basingstoke Boxing Club 113
Basingstoke Canal 7
Basingstoke Caribbean Association 113
Basingstoke Co-operative Clothing Stores 10
Basingstoke Co-operative Junior Choir 83
Basingstoke Co-operative Society *passim; see also* PIMCO
  advice on starting 11,12
  branches
    Aldermaston 52,97; Andover 104,112; Hartley Wintney 3,37,47,52,70; Kingsclere 3,70,135; Odiham 72,73, 123, 124; Overton 3,5,34,52,70,72,111,121-2,135; Tadley 97, 111,119,123,127
  candidate for Town Council 50
  country members 22,36
  customers 29
  exhibition 2,16,59
  farm 116
  flour and bread usage 22
  logos 4
  meetings 2,11,12,13,14,15,16,17,20,21,22,23,24, 25, 26,35,36,37,38,40,47,81
  membership 2,6,18,48,49,69,104,133-4
  printing works 116
  relations with other traders 11,12,20
  staff 47,56,59,60,61,64,74,82,84,92,95,110,111,112;   mess room 60; social club 60,83,85; training 125; vacancies 106; working conditions 30,60
Basingstoke Co-operative Stores 3,19
Basingstoke Town Council elections 50
Battledown Farm 1
Beggarwood Lane 123
book-keeping 62,70
Bosley, Paul (BTH 063) 58,95,110-12,118
Brambly(s) Meadow 35
Brian, Mary (BTH 081) 79,97,103
Brighton Hill 116
British Workman, The (restaurant) 11,12,13,51
Brook St 2,3,14,15,20; Lower Brook St 12,67
Brookvale Community Association 113
Buckskin 121,125; Community Centre 121
Budd's Meadow 55
builders: Goodall, H 41; John Musselwhite & Son 43,56,57,60,64
Bull, Lisette (BAHS 066) 48
butchery 8,12,39,40,48,56,60,71,74,79,82,89,94,96, 132

C

cafeteria 108
Candy, Gwen (M 141) 70,76
Carr, David 127
Carstens, Jako 125-6
cashier/cash office/finance office 75,76
Castle Field 53
Central Hall 59
charities 6,17,36,49,52,98,99,103,109,114,122,123, 124,127,129,133-4
chemists 77,82,92,96
children's festivals 4,15,26,27,35,36,38,42,47,48, 51,53,54-5
china, glass and cutlery showroom 91,94
Church Cottage 51
Church Lane 11
cinema (Plaza) 81,95,110
Clarke, Anne 4,71-2
coal 14,20,35,38,59,65,70,111; depot 67, 82
Cole, Peter 123,125
community dividend 119
competition 16,17,35,45,62,77,79,88,116,135
Connor, Criss 77,128
convenience stores 5,120,127,135
Cooper, Lynne 89

Co-operative Bank 1,35,50,68,74
Co-operative Group, The 6,125-6
Co-operative House 5,85-6,90-4,105,108,115,116,135
Co-operative Insurance Society 68
Co-operative Movement, The 1,3,8,11,13,16,17,21,
    35,37,52;.60,98,125 and politics 50.51; attacks on
    3; fair trade 6; "green" projects 6; overseas
    links 49;   Rochdale Pioneers 6,7,127
Co-operative News, The 23
Co-operative Party, The 51,104,127
Co-operative Society educational fund 15,27,37;
    educational committee 17,37,98
Co-operative Union, The 15,50,82
Co-operative Wholesale Society *see* CWS
Co-operative Women's Guild 4,6,17,23,34,52,68,97,
    98-104,114,118; evening branch 103
"Co-op rooms, The" 113
Corn Exchange 7,8
Coronation Hall *see* Masonic Hall
CWS 2,4,7,8,13,16,18,19,35,43,45,46,50,59,63

D

dairy 2,39,40,42,57-8,60,62,72,82
deliveries 1,4,25,34,36,47,56,58,61,62,66,70,71-2,
    73-4,88,89,95109,111-2,118
Denman, Gavin 128-9
Despatch/dispatch 4,23,24,29,40,62,66,71-2
directories 7,17,60,67,68,82,89
dividend ("divi") 1,2,4,7,11,12,13,17,20,35,62,68,70,
    78,105,121,133; number 42,54,74,75,76; stamps
    4,97,102-4,107,108,111
Dolan, Pauline 89
donations 48-9,121,127
drapery 36,40,41,51,7
Drill Hall 16,20,22,49,81

E

electrical goods 90,91,96,111
Eli Lilly 53,65
Elmswood Parade/Way 89
Employees Cricket Club 60,84; Debating Society 60
entertainment 15,18,20,22,53,83,85
Essex Rd 3,5,14,15,16,17,23-4,34,39-42, 45,46,
    47,51.53-5,56,57-8, 62,66,67,70,71,72,74,75,76,
    77,79,82,83,84,86,104,113,135

F

fashion 4,45,91,92
Festival Place 120
food hall 91,117
footwear 78,82,91,99
Fort Hill School 125-6
Funeralcare 5,6,128-9,133
furnishing/ furniture 2,4, 5,8,36,41,43,59,67,81,86,
    90,94,110-111,112,116,118,128,135; *see also*
    Sarum Hill, Homemaker

G

Goldings (Park, later War Memorial Park) 36,47,
    48,49
goods yard 67,82
Griffiths, Winifred 3,28-33,37
grocery 2,5,12,23,24,29-31,38,41,42,43,47,48,62,67,
    71,74,76,79,82,89,93,96,109,116,126,135

H

hair boutique 105
Harrow Way 85
Hayward, Margaret 74,83,93
Herriard 22
Hobbs, Joan (BAHS 142) 4,70,71,85,92
Homemaker, (Winklebury) 118,135
Hook 22,73
hours 8,48,71,89

I

International Meat Co 45
investments 94,107

J

John Mares 55
Jordans Nurseries 85
Junction Rd 12

K

Kelly, Jo (BAHS 066/041) 6,13,121,129,133-4
Kelvin Hughes 53,65
King's Rd *see* South Ham

L

Labour Hall 85,104
Ladies' Co-operative Supply Association 9
Lansing Bagnalls 69
Large, Barbara 24
laundry 108
Leatherby, Anita 21
Lysaght, Hazel 88-9

M

Malls, The 115
Masonic Hall 16,25,81,111
May St 12,24,26,74
Mayors 2,8,11,14,60,64,76,77,81,99
meeting places 11,12,13,15,16,20,22,23,25,51,59,
    81,104
men's wear 78,93
Merdler, Ted 133
Metcalf, Catherine (BTH 029) 74
Milestones Museum 7,78,130-131
milk 4,7,39,42,55,57-8,62,70,72,73,79,89,124
milkman 58,62,70,72,84,89,109,131
Millar, Phyl (BAHS 134) 48,66,79
Mussellwhite, Joan (BTH 054) 56
mutuality 4,51,70,127

N

Needham, Joy 8
New St 3,5,40,43-4,46,51,53,59,60,62,67,75,77,78,
    82,85,86,90-94,91,96,103,107,108,111,115,116,
    117,118,135
Newtown 12,135

O

Oakridge 72,79,82,97,103,135
off-licences 97,108
Old Basing Children's Home 53
opening hours 48
optician 77
order book 61,71,75,89
outings 38,89,134

137

overhead cash system 42,76

P
Park Prewett Hospital 89
Pavilion, 49
Peacock, Glenys 59
Penrith Rd 34,104
PIMCO 5,10,16,17,70,75,99,104-5,116,119,130-131, 135; centenary 107; 125th anniversary 119
Plummer, George 10
politics 3,32,37,50,51,104,127
Portsea Island Mutual Co-operative Society *see* PIMCO
Potter's Lane 11,51
Premises *see* Brook St, Buckskin, Co-operative House, Elmswood Parade/Way, Essex Rd, goods yard, Homemaker (Winklebury), New St, Oakridge, Sarum Hill, Soper Grove, South Ham, Vista, Winchester St, Winklebury (Centre/Way), Worting Rd (proposed)
prices 2,17,29,30,35,45,62,75,76,96,107,115,117
Provident Club 20

Q
Queen's Parade 59,77

R
Rainbow Flag, The 52,85
Rapson, Dan 124-5
rationing 66-8,69
Reading Co-operative Society 11,171
rebranding 5
relations with other traders 3,2,16,20,35
restaurant 84,103,108
Roman Rd post office 89
roundsmen 71

S
Sainsbury's 116,117,124
sales 78,90,93,105,116
sales figures 13,20,22,35,82
Sanders, Kath (BAHS 017) 72-3
Sarum Hill 5,16,20,27,53,49,,55,81,86,90,94,95-6, 107,110-112,135
saving 2,12,20,35,37,107
Seal, Joy (BAHS 056) 54-5
self-service 30,62,75,88,93,109
Sherborne House 27,38
shoes 21,36,88,93 *and see* footwear
shopping 75
Sim, Jan 120
slaughterhouse 60
Soper Grove 82,96,112
South Ham 5,60,72,79,82,88-9,135
South View 112,135
Southern Co-operative Laundries Ltd 108
Southern Co-operative(s), The 5,7,114,119-120,121-2,123,124,128,130,132,133
Southern Rd 85
special offers 1,78,93,109,115
Steele, Bernard (BTH 042) 5,121-2,132
stock-taking 66,89
Stoessel, Michelle 127
supermarkets 1,5,116,117,120,121,135

T
Tesco's 116.117
Thornycrofts 28,52,65
tokens 4,36,62,70,72,79,89
Toop, Ken and Lil (M 043) 2,47,61-2,75
"Top of the Town, The" 62,89,107,116
Town Centre, new 5,116,117,120,135
town expansion/growth 5,46,85,90,135
Town Hall 48,58,60,83,85,89; (new) 8
traders (other than Co-op) 8 *see* directories
Trade(s) Unions 15,21,50,60
Traynor, Gerry 76
treats *see* children's festivals
typhoid epidemic 11

U
undertakers 128 *and see* Funeralcare

V
Venture Bus Company 39
Vicarage meadow 26
Vista 5,117,120,135
Voluntary Co-operative Party 104
Vyne Rd Boys' Home 53

W
wages 17,20,21,60,71,76,95
Walkers' Stores 33
Wallis & Steevens 9, 11,28,65
War Memorial Park *see* Goldings (Park)
Wellington Social Club 89
Wheatsheaf paddock 27,35
White, Tilly (BAHS 144) 1
Williams, Ian 16
Winchester St 5,6,52,60,67,68,78,82,85,86,96,128
Winklebury 5,7,89,99,109,118,135; Centre 109;Way 125-6
Women's Co-operative Guild 15,17,23,32,51-2,85,98 *see also* Co-operative Women's Guild
women, role of 4,10,13,15,17,29,31-3,34,35,37,46, 51,112
workhouse 53
workmen's cottages 15
Worting Rd (proposed shops) 60
Wright, Pat (BAHS 095) 55
WW1 3,29-38
WW2 3,65-8